INTERNATIONAL BUSINESS TOPICS

David Cotton

Nelson

Thomas Nelson and Sons Limited
Nelson House   Mayfield Road
Walton-on-Thames   Surrey
KT12 5PL   UK

51 York Place
Edinburgh
EH1 3JD   UK

Thomas Nelson (Hong Kong) Limited
Toppan Buildings 10/F
22A Westlands Road
Quarry Bay   Hong Kong

First published by Evans Brothers Limited 1980
(Under ISBN 0-237-50279-8)
Reprinted three times

Second impression published by Unwin Hyman 1984
(Under ISBN 0-7135-2398-0)
Reprinted four times

Third impression published by Thomas Nelson and Sons Limited 1989

ISBN 0-17-555822-1
NPN 9 8 7 6

Acknowledgements

The publishers are grateful to the following for permission to reproduce
photographs and drawings on the pages indicated: Camera Press Ltd, pages
14, 15, 45, 116 (photograph by Armand Latourre), 117 (photograph by Francois
Chalais); Associated Newspapers Group Ltd, pages 23, 24, 31 and 44 (cartoon
by Jon); Radio Times Hulton Picture Library, page 30; The Sun, page 46; The
World Bank, pages 61 and 62 (World Bank Photos by Kay Muldoon and Ray
Witlin); Govan Shipbuilders Ltd, page 70; *De Telegraaf*, pages 76 and 78;
Costain International Ltd, page 84; Henk Snoek, page 85; London Express
Pictures, pages 92; Hong Kong Preventive Service, page 102; The New York
Stock Exchange, page 131; Barclays, page 136 (photograph by Walter
Nurnberg); *The Sunday Times*, page 138; Georg Sessler/Bildhuset, pages 143 and
144; Dick Jordan/Bronze Records Ltd, page 151; Australian Information
Service, pages 152 and 154 (photograph by Michael Jensen).

The Language Practice exercise on page 67 is extracted from an article 'Hamish
McRae talks to Robert MacNamara' by Hamish McRae, printed in *The Guardian*.
The Language Practice exercise on page 88 is extracted from an article
'Expatriate Life' by Bryn Williams printed in the *Financial Times*, March 1977.

The cartoons, except those on the pages indicated above, were drawn by Ron
McTrusty. Illustrations © Unwin Hyman Limited.

Picture research by Enid Moore.

Printed in Great Britain by
Scotprint Ltd, Musselburgh.

Contents

Introduction

What is 'International Business Topics'?

This book comprises a selection of reading texts dealing with topical, and often controversial, business issues. The word 'international' is a true reflection of the wide-ranging content of the material. Some of the topics relate to problems of a particular country. In this category are texts with titles such as: Construction Contracts in Saudi Arabia; The Japanese Approach to Business: Venezuela's Oil Revenues; India versus Coca Cola and IBM. Other articles are, by their very nature, international in scope. One thinks of such titles as: Multinationals; The World Bank; Bribery; National Stereotypes.

Taken as a whole, the texts give the student a great deal of information about what is really happening in the business world — the significant trends, the important new ideas — and they encourage the reader to examine critically business practices and institutions in his or her own country.

Those people who already have a good command of English will probably gain most benefit from the book. That is why *International Business Topics* has been graded as advanced level. However, an intermediate-level student who is intelligent and interested in business can cope with the topics, especially if a teacher is present to give guidance. Although the texts are designed principally for class-instruction, some students will wish to use them for self-instruction. To meet the need of this group, a key to most of the exercises is provided at the back of the book.

The main aims of *International Business Topics* are:

a) to develop reading skills and give practice in the comprehension of business texts;

b) to improve the student's command of vocabulary, specialist terms and idiomatic language commonly used in business;

c) to provide students with an opportunity to practise their spoken English, and above all, to encourage them to analyze and discuss ideas by presenting them with intellectually-challenging material;

d) to offer other language activities, for example, grammatical exercises and writing assignments, which will help those studying at high-intermediate and advanced levels to improve their language skills.

Organization of the book

Each topic contains: (i) preparation for the text; (ii) the text; (iii) language notes; (iv) exercises linked to each passage, giving practice in the various language skills.

In the Preparation section, there are two or three questions about the subject matter of the text. The purpose of these is to start the student thinking about the topic and to generate some preliminary discussion. While reading the passage, the student will be looking for the answers to the questions he or she has been asked.

The extent of the Language Notes depends on the number and type of terms that need to be explained or commented on. Generally, the items consist of expressions which may not be in the student's dictionary — they may, for example, be too specialized — or of colloquial language whose meaning the student may not readily understand. Grammatical difficulties or problems of usage may also be discussed in this section.

Exploitation of the ideas and language of the texts is organized in sections. These are:

Section A	Comprehension
Section B	Vocabulary
Section C	Language Practice
Section D	Oral Work
Section E	Writing Exercises

The wide margins provide some space for students to write down their answers and/or notes for most sections.

Section A   Comprehension
Generally, this comprises about 6–8 questions which test how well the reader has understood the main ideas of the text.

Section B   Vocabulary
This concentrates on vocabulary development. Some exercises are based on words and phrases in the text itself, and they test whether the student has grasped the precise meaning of these terms; other exercises introduce new vocabulary which is in some way related to the topic. The section also includes work on idiomatic expressions. In order to provide variety, several different types of vocabulary exercises are used: multiple choice, filling blanks, finding synonyms, changing the form of words, etc.

Section C   Language Practice
In this section, there are exercises which give practice in areas of grammar and usage. These are not presented sequentially according to some arbitrary standard of difficulty. The aim is simply to give the student practice with the kind of language work which is often useful at high-intermediate and advanced levels. Thus, some exercises deal with difficult verb tenses, verb patterns and modal auxiliaries; others focus on conjunctions, use of the article, prepositions or phrasal verbs.

Section D   Oral Work
Here, students are given the opportunity to discuss ideas in the text, and also to defend their own point of view concerning an aspect of the topic. In most of the sections, one or two debating themes are given. These are deliberately worded to evoke controversy and to encourage the student to speak persuasively for or against the motion in question. In addition to the themes, there are discussion topics and role-playing exercises.

3

Section E   Writing Exercises
In most of the texts, there are some essay topics of the traditional type. The student is required to write discursively on given subjects closely related to what he or she has just read. However, there are a number of other written assignments involving the writing of letters, reports, telexes and press releases. In most cases, there is also the opportunity for the student to practise writing a summary.

How to use the texts

The experienced teacher will obviously adopt whatever approach is most suited to the needs of the class and the teaching time available. The suggestions which follow are intended as a guide only.

Advanced-level classes
1. Invite students to select topics which they think would interest them.
2. Having chosen a topic, complete the Preparation section in class.
3. Ideally, the reading of the text and sections A and B (Comprehension and Vocabulary) should be carried out as a homework assignment. If this is not possible, these sections can be done in class time under the guidance of the teacher.
4. The teacher takes up points in the Language Notes and discusses these with the class.
5. Either section C (Language Practice) or section D (Oral Work) should now follow. In practice, classes often wish, at this stage, to discuss the topic. In this case, section D will precede Section C.
6. Section E should now be dealt with. Because of limitations of time, the teacher may choose one particular written assignment for the class. Alternatively, some teachers may prefer to let students choose themselves.

Intermediate-level classes
The same approach as that outlined above may be used, but the teacher may find it more useful to read the text with the class and deal with language difficulties as they arise.

Final comments

International Business Topics is meant to be the kind of book which will not only be used by teachers and students in the classroom but which will also be read with enjoyment by those who are studying privately at home.

In selecting texts for inclusion in the book, the author has searched for topics dealing with important activities and events in the business world. He has then tried to encourage the reader to think about and discuss the ideas in the texts. As a result, this book is designed not so much for readers possessing a certain level of language competence, but rather for any intelligent student who is genuinely interested in business and is therefore willing to make the effort to understand the material which is presented.

Multinationals

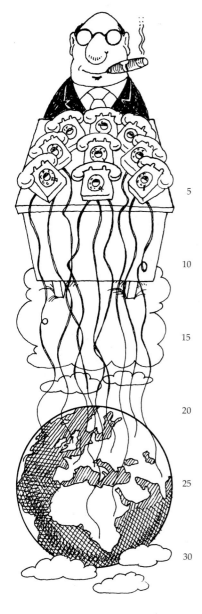

Preparation

1. What is a multinational company?
2. Which multinationals have subsidiaries in your own country?
3. Why do the governments of some countries encourage multinationals to set up production or sales facilities in their midst while others discourage this type of foreign investment?

The term 'multinational' is used for a company which has subsidiaries or sales facilities throughout the world. Another expression for this type of business enterprise is 'global corporation'. Many of these giant organizations are household names such as Coca
5 Cola, Heinz, Sony, Hitachi, IBM, Akzo and General Motors. Companies like these control vast sums of money and they operate in countries with widely differing political and economic systems.

Looking back into history, we can find two main reasons for the development of multinationals. Firstly, when companies found that
10 their national markets had become saturated, they realized that they could only increase profits by setting up subsidiaries abroad. Secondly, if a country set up trade barriers — usually tariffs or quotas — against a company's products, then the only alternative for the company was to establish a factory or sales organization in the
15 country concerned.

More recently, the economic boom of the 1960s led to a rapid growth of globe-trotting enterprises. In the highly industrialized countries rising incomes attracted the multinationals; in the developing countries, the availability of cheap labour lured many
20 companies into building new factories and assembly plants.

In earlier times, most countries gave the multinationals a 'red carpet' welcome because they saw such foreign investment as creating much-needed employment, stimulating the business sector generally, and possibly earning foreign currency if the company's
25 products were exported. More recently, however, the tide has turned against the multinationals. They are now viewed by many with suspicion; once heroes, they are now villains on the international business stage.

For reasons outlined below, host countries are now restricting the
30 activities of their guests, the multinationals. Many developing countries will only allow new investment if it is on a joint-venture basis. This means that local entrepreneurs, or state agencies, must participate in the ownership and even management of the foreign enterprise. Other countries, e.g. India and Nigeria, are forcing
35 foreign companies already well-established to reduce their shareholdings to a certain percentage, say 60% or 40% of the total equity of the company.

At international level, various attempts have been made to regulate the activities of the multinational. The most gentlemanly of these has
40 been the OECD[1]'s guidelines on multinationals: a kind of book of

---

1. Organization for Economic
   Cooperation and Development.

5

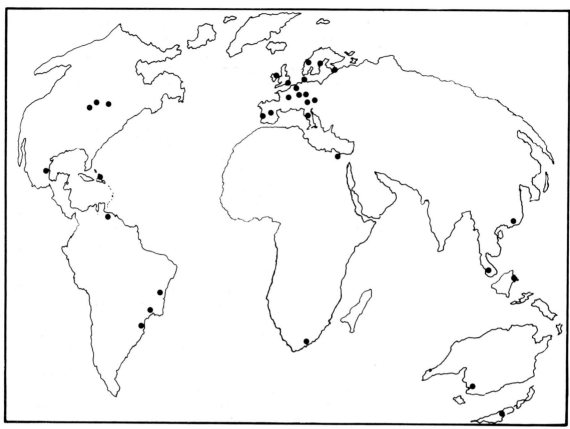

The extent of only one company's operations is indicated on this map: each dot marks a subsidiary of the parent company, the Ford Motor Company.

etiquette advising companies how to behave in public. The code, being voluntary, is not legally enforceable.

Tension between host country and multinational is inevitable in many cases because multinationals do pose a threat to national
45 sovereignty.

The multinational is big and rich. It often operates in industries which are difficult to enter and of vital national importance, e.g. the computer, chemical and automobile industries. Most important of all, the main objective of the multinational is to organize its activities
50 around the world so as to maximize global profits and global market shares. Each subsidiary is part of an international network of affiliates. These all interact with each other. Each part serves the whole. The centre controlling the network — the multinationals' headquarters — is not under the control of the host government. It is
55 frequently thousands of miles away from these subsidiaries.

To illustrate this principle of interaction between affiliates, we can take the example of the Canadian company, Massey Ferguson. It can make tractors in the USA for sale in Canada that contain British engines, French transmissions and Mexican axles: all products of the
60 company's subsidiaries. IBM is another company which is transnational in scope. A typical 360-series computer may include components from four or five countries.

To show how a multinational plans and operates internationally, let us take the case of SKF[2], a Swedish ball-bearing manufacturer. When

2. Aktiefolaget Svenska · Kullagerfabriker.

65 it took over its Italian affiliate RIV in 1965, RIV was entirely
    dependent on the Italian market. It was also near collapse because it
    had overestimated demand for its products and was suffering from
    overcapacity. SKF immediately started feeding it with export orders
    and continued until the domestic market picked up again. RIV then
70 concentrated on the domestic market and the export orders were
    reduced.
        Increasingly, in recent years, governments have had to ask
    themselves whether multinationals are harming their national
    interests. In highly industrialized countries, a major source of worry
75 has been that these foreign giants will take over smaller companies
    and gradually dominate an important industry. If this happens, vital
    decisions affecting the economic interests of the country may be
    taken in boardrooms thousands of miles away from that country.
        The danger of this kind of domination is perfectly exemplified by a
80 controversial takeover which occurred in France. In 1966, the French
    computer company Machines-Bull had 66% of its stock bought up by
    General Electric. This meant in effect that France no longer had its
    own computer industry. As a result, the French government felt
    bound to set up its own data processing and computer concern which
85 cooperated closely with the German company Siemens and the Dutch
    company Philips.
        Undoubtedly, governments are uneasy when they feel that
    decisions affecting plants and employment in their countries are
    being made by remote control. Furthermore, unions often feel that
90 their bargaining power is weakened when they have to deal with
    people operating from remote decision centres.
        Developing countries, in particular, have become concerned about
    their dependence on foreign investment in key sectors of their
    economy. They have become aware that foreign subsidiaries often
95 take most of their profits out of the country rather than reinvest them
    in the company. Sometimes, the flow of funds causes disastrous
    fluctuations in the exchange rates of their currencies. Certain
    countries have accused the multinationals of political interference.
    The classic case of this is, of course, the intrusion of ITT
100 (International Telegraph and Telephones) in the political affairs of
    Chile. This huge conglomerate, involved in every area of industrial
    and banking activity, was ready to finance attempts to overthrow the
    Marxist government of the Communist leader, Salvador Allende.
        To gain greater control over their industry, some countries, as
105 already mentioned, are beginning to insist on joint ventures. The
    disadvantage of this tactic is that the foreign subsidiary may then be
    treated less favourably, in terms of technical assistance and capital
    investment, by the parent company.
        Another strategy used by governments is to limit the amount of
110 profits that a foreign subsidiary may repatriate in a given period.
        Arguing against multinationals, critics cry in shrill tones that these
    organizations engage in anti-competitive activities, insensitively shut
    down plants, make huge bribes to gain contracts, interfere politically,
    destabilize currencies, underpay their workers and so on. Those
115 speaking for the defence see these corporations almost as
    international agencies, promoting peace, providing better, cheaper
    products, and bringing much needed resources, expertise and
    employment to the host countries.

Language Notes

Line 4   *Household names:* names familiar to almost everyone.

Line 7   *Economic:* note the different meanings of *economic* and *economical*.

        Examples: 'The economic situation of our country is good.' (Material prosperity)

        'She is an economical housewife.' (Not wasteful, thrifty)

Line 11   *Set up:* a company sets up or establishes subsidiaries/factories/plants abroad.

Line 16   *Economic boom:* a sudden increase in business activity. When business activity declines sharply, the term used is *slump*.

Line 21   *Red carpet welcome:* more usually 'to give someone the red carpet treatment'. To welcome warmly and to give lavish hospitality. Presidents and Prime Ministers, when travelling abroad, are usually given the red carpet treatment.

Line 61   *Scope:* range, e.g. 'The scope of his thesis is very wide'.

Line 65   *Took over:* took control of. In this context, note the phrase *takeover bid*, i.e. an offer by one company to buy the stock of another and so control it, e.g. 'Company X made a takeover bid for Company Y.'

Line 69   *Domestic market:* home market. Contrast this term with a company's *foreign* or *overseas* markets.

Line 81   *Bought up:* the sense of *up* is *all* or *as much/many as possible*.

Line 84   *Bound to:* an obligation to.

Line 92   *Concerned about:* worried about. Note the difference in meaning between: *concerned about* (worried about), *concerned in* (involved in).

        Examples: 'I am concerned about my health.'

        'He was concerned in many financial ventures.'

Line 99   *Classic case:* perfect example.

Line 111   *Critics:* a critic is a person who criticizes or judges someone or something. He writes criticism.

Line 113   *Interfere:* interfere *in* someone's business or affairs, but interfere *with* something.

Line 117   *Expertise:* expert knowledge. *Know-how* is an alternative expression.

A Comprehension

1. What are some of the main characteristics of multinational companies?
2. Host countries used to look upon the multinationals as 'heroes'. Why?
3. The writer describes the OECD guidelines to multinationals as a *gentlemanly* attempt to regulate their activities. Why does he use the word *gentlemanly* and what tone does he employ? (1.39–42)

4. Multinationals have been described as having an organic structure. In what sense is this an appropriate expression for the way they are organized?

5. What point is the writer trying to make when discussing the case of SKF's Italian affiliate RIV? (l.63–71)

6. Complete this sentence. The French government felt it had to set up its own data processing and computer concern because ...... (l.79–86)

7. Multinationals have been accused of decision-making by *remote control*. What does this phrase mean? State briefly some of the problems that can arise from this practice.

8. Some governments have begun to insist that foreign companies can only operate in their country on a joint venture basis. What can be gained and lost by such a policy towards foreign investment?

B Vocabulary

1. Find an appropriate word for each blank space. In all sections the initial letter of each word is provided.

   a) Most multinational companies are vast enterprises with networks of s...... or a...... throughout the world. Originally they expanded overseas because trade barriers such as t...... and q...... had been set up against their goods.

   b) When incomes are rising and business is thriving, in other words, when there is an e...... b...... in a country, a multinational may decide to establish a subsidiary there. Later, however, the government of the country may only allow the company to operate on a j...... v...... basis, in which case it will compel the company to reduce its s...... to a fixed percentage. It could even restrict the subsidiary by allowing only a fixed proportion of profits to be r...... .

   c) The OECD code gave g...... on how multinationals should behave. None of its provisions were l...... e......, and therefore some say it lacked legal teeth.

   d) A factory whose production resources are not being fully utilized is said to be suffering from o...... .

2. Complete each sentence using an appropriate form of the word in *italics*.
   Example:
   profit   This is one of our most *profitable* product lines.

   a) *enterprise*   What we need at the moment is an ...... manager.

   b) *differ*   The two products look, taste and feel the same. It is impossible to ...... between them.

   c) *basis*   She needs more experience, but ...... she is a first-class buyer.

   d) *tension*   When I asked for an increase in salary, the atmosphere here became somewhat ....

e) *threaten* The leaking of the results of our market survey poses a serious ...... to company security.

f) *rich* The oil ...... of certain Arab states are known to all.

g) *market* Our sales director doubts whether this ingenious but complex toy is really ....

h) *worry* The lack of job opportunities for young people is very ....

i) *decision* Hesitant! Vacillating! Never making up his mind! What an ...... chairman.

j) *remote* It is not ...... possible that I shall become head of this department.

k) *intrusion* A good chairman in a meeting should not be too ....

l) *involve* Unfortunately, our ...... in this deal has now become public knowledge.

m) *strategy* This area is of great ...... importance in our promotional campaign.

3. Circle the number next to the most appropriate answer.

a) When a market becomes *saturated* (l.10):
   (i) it allows a new company to enter easily and quickly.
   (ii) it offers no potential for a company to develop its sales.
   (iii) it immediately begins to attract foreign investment.

b) *Globe-trotting enterprises* (l.17) are those which:
   (i) prefer to operate in foreign markets rather than domestic ones.
   (ii) seek to expand their business activities by setting up organizations abroad.
   (iii) believe that greater profits are to be earned abroad than in their own countries.

c) The best definition of a *developing country* is that:
   (i) it is at a very high level of economic and social development.
   (ii) it is still in the process of becoming a highly industrialized nation.
   (iii) it is still at a stage well below its maximum economic potential.

d) One difference between a *conglomerate* and an *affiliate* is that the former:
   (i) usually has a more complex organization and engages in diverse business activities.
   (ii) is always more stable financially and more profitable.
   (iii) is a large organization which only engages in international trading.

e) If multinationals *insensitively shut down plants* (l.112):
   (i) they have no intention of compensating the workers of these plants.

    (ii) they make such decisions without consulting the
government of the host country.

    (iii) they pay little attention to the interests of those in the host
country.

C Language Practice

1. Use the groups of words in their given order and make meaningful
sentences.

Example:
Many/these corporations/household names/Heinz, Coca Cola
— *Many of these corporations are household names such as Heinz and Coca Cola.*

a) Companies/national markets/become saturated/often
decide/subsidiaries abroad.

b) Economic boom/1960s/led/rapid growth/multinational activity.

c) In earlier times/multinationals/considered/heroes/but
now/view/suspicion.

d) Many countries/only allow/foreign investment/joint-venture
basis.

e) Some people regard multinationals/threat/national sovereignty.

f) Some developing countries/concerned/dependence/foreign
investment/key sectors/economy.

g) ITT/American conglomerate/accused/interfering/political
affairs/Chile.

h) The principle/interaction/well exemplified/company/Massey
Ferguson.

2. Rewrite each of the following groups of sentences as **one** complex
sentence. Do **not** use *and*, *but* or *because*. Make any necessary
changes or additions.

Example:
Multinationals should be prevented from bribing government
officials. A code should be devised to achieve this aim. This is
vital.
— *It is vital that a code should be devised to prevent multinationals
from bribing government officials.*

a) Multinationals were once considered heroes. They are now
regarded as villains. This is somewhat surprising.

b) Foreign companies may have good intentions. They may have
bad intentions. Their activities will inevitably be closely
scrutinized by host governments.

c) General Electric bought up the French company Machines-Bull.
France no longer had a computer industry. This worried many
Frenchmen.

11

d) SKF took over the Italian company RIV. It immediately started feeding RIV with export orders. The aim was to help the Italian company recover financially.

e) Governments are not happy about decisions being made by remote control. These decisions often affect plants and employment. Unions also are not pleased. They fear their power may be weakened.

D Oral Work

1. Role Play

   A television broadcasting organization has invited *a small group of multinational executives* to participate in a panel discussion. They are to start the ball rolling by speaking in support of the following debating theme:

   'Multinationals are, on balance, a force for good in the world and strong restrictions on their activities are unnecessary.'

   A critical studio audience has been assembled to challenge the views of the executives.

   A neutral chairman will guide the discussion. *An eminent politician* will listen to the debate, sum up at the end, and choose the most effective group — executives or studio audience.

   A studio manager will organize the debaters and will have the right to speak when necessary.

   Enact this television debate.

2. Discussion Topics

   a) What are the advantages of working for a large multinational company rather than for an organization which operates in one country only?

   b) Choose two or three world-famous multinational companies operating in your country. What kind of reputation does each of them enjoy? Could the 'image' of any company be improved?

E Writing Exercises

1. 'Multinational companies may possibly have some part to play in the economic life of underdeveloped and developing nations. It is highly doubtful, however, that in developed, highly industrialized countries, these companies bring enough benefits to offset their harmful activities.'

   Discuss this statement, illustrating your arguments with examples.

2. A foreign magazine specializing in current affairs has asked you to send a short article about a multinational company which operates in your country. Write this article, including any information that you think might interest the foreign reader in the country concerned.

India versus Coca Cola and IBM

Preparation

1. What are some of the similarities and differences between the two companies, Coca Cola and IBM (International Business Machines)?
2. In what ways might India benefit from the presence of these two companies in the country?
3. What types of foreign investment might be useful for a country like India?

In an ideal world, most multinational companies, and especially American-owned ones, would prefer to retain 100% control over their subsidiaries throughout the world. Full ownership enables them to plan and manage operations on an integrated basis, to maximize
5 economies of scale, and to move components across national borders without having to be sensitive to the special needs of local shareholders.

Some countries, especially in the developing world, have taken measures to <u>compel</u> multinationals to enter into partnership with
10 local investors. In Nigeria, for example, the government's 'Indigenization' decree has forced many foreign companies to accept increasing Nigerian participation in the ownership of their companies. In India, a similar policy towards foreign investment is being followed, and the 'Indianization' of their industry is being
15 achieved by means of the Foreign Exchange Regulation Act of 1973.

It was this act which, in 1977, led to a dramatic confrontation between the Indian government on the one hand, and the two multinationals Coca Cola and IBM, on the other. After tough negotiations, the trial of strength resulted in both companies pulling
20 out of India.

The act requires foreign companies to dilute their foreign equity shareholdings to 40%, this process being carried out in stages. The foreign company, therefore, has to reorganize its Indian operations to allow majority local ownership.
25 In the case of Coca Cola, the dispute arose because of the company's refusal to fall into line with the Foreign Exchange Regulation Act (FERA).

The main point of issue concerned the formula for making coca cola. For over 91 years, this has been a closely guarded secret. Also,
30 the Coca Cola company had had a long-standing policy of supervising the manufacture of the concentrate from which the drink was made, and this had applied to plants in the US and overseas.

If the Coca Cola company had complied with the act, it would have had to divulge the secret formula of its concentrate. At that time, the
35 Indian bottling plants imported the concentrate through a Delhi-based company which received supplies from the parent company.

Under the act, the Coca Cola company would have had to set up an Indian company in which the foreign equity would not exceed 40%.

13

tinge

40 This new firm would have taken over all Coca Cola's operations in India — including the supply of the concentrate.

During the protracted negotiations, Coca Cola offered to increase its exports of other commodities from India to make up for the foreign exchange that it spent on the concentrate. Nevertheless, the

45 government insisted that Coca Cola transferred to the proposed Indian company all its activities, including the technical know-how and blending operations of the concentrate.

The closure of the Coca Cola plant left 22 Indian-owned bottling

A well-stocked stall . . .

. . . but in spite of the advertisements,
the water-pipe remains the most
important source of refreshment.

factories idle and thousands of workers unemployed. To remedy this
50 situation, the government planned to manufacture a Coca Cola
substitute which was being developed by its food research
laboratories. This would be supplied to manufacturers. One idea was
to call it '77' to mark the year that Coca Cola fell from grace! While the
Indian government was optimistic about the potential of the new soft
55 drink, most experts took the view that it was impossible to duplicate
exactly the ingredients of coca cola, since minute quantities of these
affect its taste.

IBM fell out with the Indian government for different reasons. This
company has a global policy that all its subsidiaries in other countries
60 must be fully US owned; also, it does not establish factories in
countries where it is not allowed to market its products.

To get round the provisions of the Foreign Exchange Regulation
Act, IBM tried to bargain with the Indian government. IBM wanted to
retain 100% ownership of a plant which would export all the
65 computers which it manufactured in India. It also agreed to set up
another Indian majority-owned company to service existing IBM
machines. It continued, however, to demand the right to import
modern IBM machines for its Indian customers. This turned out to be
the major stumbling block to agreement with the Indian government.
70 An important opponent to IBM in India was India's department of
electronics. It argued that no special concessions should be allowed to
IBM. It calculated that if IBM was required to sell in India computers
manufactured in the country itself, rather than import them, there
would be a 40% saving in foreign exchange costs on this item.
75 Another argument used was that other computer companies,
including Britain's ICL, had already toed the line regarding dilution
of ownership.

IBM, like Coca Cola, found that it could not budge the Indian government which probably took a hard line because it feared that,
80 once it started making concessions to powerful multinationals, its whole policy towards foreign investment would be undermined. For its part, by pulling out of India, IBM upheld its principle of operating independently.

The exit from India of these two companies was dramatic and
85 caused a stir internationally, but they were not the only ones to pull out as a result of FERA. About 670 foreign companies were asked to dilute their holdings, and at least 52 companies wound up their operations rather than comply with the act.

Some companies were allowed, under the act, to keep a majority
90 share providing that they diversified into agreed fields coming under the category of 'sophisticated technology' or 'export'. They really had to propose an acceptable package combining these categories. Some firms managed to do just this. Union Carbide, for example, set up a deep-sea fishing unit aimed solely at export markets. Most companies
95 fell into line either by diversifying their activities or by 'Indianizing'. They probably reasoned, 'Half a loaf is better than none'. After all, India was probably the most important third world market in which many of them had a stake.

Was IBM wise to stick to its principles? Should it perhaps have
100 taken a pragmatic position like most other companies who had obviously been swayed by the importance of India as a market? If IBM continues this policy, it might be squeezed out of large areas of the world, leaving markets free for more flexible competitors. *give rise to concern*

On the other hand, would India's tough approach create anxiety in
105 other foreign investors, and thereby reduce the flow of investment funds? The Minister of Industry stated quite clearly after the showdown with IBM that India welcomed foreign investment in areas of sophisticated technology, production designed to boost exports, and in high priority sectors, but, he added, such foreign expertise and foreign investment must be 'on our terms'.

Language Notes

Line 10	*Sensitive to*: opposite form — insensitive to.
Line 25	*Dilute*: weaken or reduce. To drink whisky, we sometimes dilute it with water.
Line 29	The dispute *arose*: the word *arise* is frequently used with words like problem, difficulty, quarrel and dispute.
	Example: 'A difficulty arose over the question of finance.'
Line 30	*To fall into line with*: to obey.
Line 36	*The* US: a few countries are preceded by *the*, e.g. the US, the USSR, the UK, the Netherlands.
Line 47	*Make up for*: compensate for. If you forget someone's birthday, try to make up for it in some way.
Line 49	The government *insisted*: we can either say:
	'The government insisted that Coca Cola transfer ......'
	transferred ......'
	or 'The government insisted on Coca Cola transferring ......'
Line 50	*Knowhow*: specialized knowledge, expertise.
Line 57	*Fell from grace*: lost the favour of the Indian government.
Line 58	*Potential*: future prospects. Often used about people, e.g.
	'He is an executive with great potential.' i.e. a very promising executive.
Line 62	*Fell out with*: quarreled, disagreed with.
Line 80	*Toed the line*: obeyed.
Line 89	*Caused a stir*: attracted a great deal of publicity. Film stars usually cause a stir when they arrive at airports.
Line 100	*Half a loaf is better than none*: it is better to compromise and gain something rather than get nothing at all.
Line 102	*Had a stake*: had business interests, e.g. 'This company has a stake in the leisure industry.' Note the idiom: *At stake*, e.g. 'This is an ambitious and risky enterprise. A lot of money is at stake.' (at risk)
Line 111	*Showdown*: frank declaration of intentions. Here, the meaning is approximately that of a *confrontation*.
Line 112	*Boost*: increase, stimulate, e.g. 'The high mark I got in my examination boosted my confidence.'

A Comprehension

1. Many countries in the developing world are adopting a similar policy towards foreign companies operating in their midst. Describe the approach they are using.
2. The Indian government would have liked the Coca Cola company to set up a new enterprise controlled by Indians. Why did Coca Cola object to the proposal?

3. Outline the main consequences to India of Coca Cola withdrawing from the country.
4. In the dispute between India and IBM, no satisfactory compromise was reached. Explain why:
   a) IBM refused to comply with the FERA act.
   b) the Indian government was unwilling to give way.
5. In about five lines, summarize the Indian government's approach to foreign investment in the country. Base your answer on information given in the topic.

B Vocabulary

1. Find an appropriate word for each blank space. In both sections, the initial letter of each word is provided.

   a) Many developing countries are forcing foreign companies to enter into p...... with local investors. As a result, the foreign company has to dilute its e...... s...... to a fixed percentage, say 60% or 40%. Some companies refuse to do this, deciding instead to p...... o...... of the country. Others negotiate with the government concerned, hoping to reach some sort of c....... .

   b) The case of Coca Cola was simple. The company did not want to c...... with the FERA act because it was unwilling to d...... the secret formula of its concentrate. IBM, on the other hand, engaged in some very hard b...... with the Indian government. The company has a global p...... of 100% ownership of its subsidiaries. Also, it does not like to s...... u...... factories in countries where it cannot m...... its products. This t...... o...... to be a major obstacle to agreement. In the end, the Indian government felt that no special c...... should be made to IBM. Many people think that IBM should have given way and been a little more f...... .

2. Complete each sentence using an appropriate form of the word in *italics*.
   Example:
   prefer   Many companies have a ...... for 100% ownership of their overseas subsidiaries.
          — Many companies have a *preference* for 100% ownership of their overseas subsidiaries.

   a) *economy*   The ...... situation of many countries will change once their oil reserves have been exhausted.

   b) *prefer*   Companies often give ...... treatment to important customers.

   c) *compel*   Finance ministers in socialist governments usually feel a ...... to impose heavy taxes on those earning high incomes.

   d) *similar*   The economic and political structures of the US and the USSR are completely ....

e) *organize*   A major strike or a fire in a plant is bound to
                       ...... production schedules.

f) *potential*   This is, ..., an excellent development project.

g) *remedy*   When a product is shown to be defective, a
                       company must take ...... measures.

h) *taste*   It was an impressive office, furnished in a most
                       ...... manner.

i) *bargain*   In a large company, ... for higher wages is
                       usually carried out by highly skilled union
                       personnel.

j) *diversify*   ...... can sometimes be a very risky business for
                       a company.

k) *flexible*   When a company's management never makes
                       concessions and always adopts an ...... attitude
                       towards its employees, it will soon have
                       industrial relations problems.

l) *confrontation*   She is the kind of person who will always work
                       harder when ...... by a challenging assignment.

3. Circle the number next to the most suitable answer.

   a) *Economies of scale* (1.9) enable companies:
      (i) to reduce the scale of their operations to a more efficient
          size.
      (ii) to achieve a more acceptable distribution of shares.
      (iii) to reduce costs by increasing the size of their operations.

   b) The Indian government and Coca Cola were engaged in
      protracted negotiations. This phrase means that:
      (i) talks between the two sides were extremely bitter.
      (ii) bargaining between negotiators on both sides was tiring.
      (iii) discussions between the government and the company
            lasted a long time.

   c) If the *blending operations of the concentrate* (1.51) were
      transferred to an Indian company, the Indians:
      (i) would be able to operate a Coca Cola bottling factory
          efficiently.
      (ii) would be ready to export Coca Cola on a large scale.
      (iii) would learn how to mix the basic ingredients of Coca
            Cola.

   d) The Indian government feared that, by giving in to IBM, its
      whole policy would be *undermined* (1.85). This word means:
      (i) weakened
      (ii) changed
      (iii) opposed

   e) This *turned out* to be a major *stumbling block* to agreement. The
      sentence can best be rewritten as follows:
      (i) This meant that agreement could only be reached after
          much stumbling.

(ii) This proved to be an important obstacle to reaching agreement.

(iii) This made it too difficult for the two sides to agree.

C Language Practice

1. Complete the following paragraphs by supplying a suitable preposition, conjunction or article for each blank space.

a) The withdrawals of the two companies were highly-publicized incidents in ...... development of ...... policies of the Indian government ...... foreign investment. ...... a result of this policy, many companies have already decided to wind ...... their operations. ......, the Indian government is in the process of asking others to follow suit.

b) A great many companies have diversified ...... areas favoured by the government. Others have 'Indianized'; they feel that, by doing ......, they will not necessarily lose control ...... their company's policy. They prefer to keep a stake ...... the country because India represents ...... large and growing market for them.

c) When developing countries bring ...... legislation to gain some degree of control over foreign companies, the companies generally react ...... the law by trying to get ...... it in some way. If they are unsuccessful, they either comply ...... the law or they end ...... by falling .... the government concerned and having a showdown with it. Such companies prefer to stick ...... their principles rather than risk allowing local investors to participate ...... their enterprise.

2. Write a second sentence which is equivalent in meaning to the one above it. Use the sentence openings provided.

Example:
Some governments have insisted on multinationals entering into partnership with local investors.
Multinationals have been made ......
— *Multinationals have been made by some governments to enter into partnership with local investors.*

a) The enforcement of the FERA act brought about a confrontation between a government and a multinational.
One consequence ......

b) To make up for the foreign exchange it spent on the concentrate, Coca Cola offered to increase its exports of other commodities.
Coca Cola suggested ......

c) While the government was optimistic about the drink's potential, many experts remained rather sceptical.
Despite ......

d) The Department of Electronics did not want special concessions to be given to IBM.
The Department of Electronics objected ......

e) These policies may seem unwise to the two multinationals, but many people support the Indian government's actions.
However ......

f) Some foreign companies managed to keep a majority share, but only if they diversified into special areas of business.
Only by ......

D Oral Work

1. Argue for or against the following debating theme:
'In the cases of the Coca Cola company and IBM, the Indian government acted not only too hastily, but also against its own short and long term interests.'

2. Role Play

You are a commercial attaché in an embassy abroad. The local Chamber of Commerce has invited you to dinner. After the dinner, you will be chairman of an informal meeting which will discuss this topic: *'Developing countries and the problems of foreign investment.'*
During the meeting, you will have before you the notes given below. You may add any other points you think could be useful. Enact this meeting with other members of your group.

Notes:
Benefits of foreign investment
a) Creation of employment opportunities.
b) Development of poor regions of a country.
c) Stimulus to business generally.
d) Export earnings.
e) Bringing technology, management and technical skills, etc.
f) Providing training for local labour.

Negative aspects of foreign investment
a) Exploitation of cheap local labour.
b) Preventing the growth of local enterprises.
c) Restricting competition by unfair trading practices or by taking over weaker local companies.
d) Repatriating profits, with effects on a country's currency — possibly destabilizing it.

E Writing Exercises

1. The Indian Minister of Industry has written to IBM saying that his Ministry will reconsider its decision regarding 'Indianization' of the company. He has asked to receive a short document (one or two pages) which restates briefly and clearly the case for IBM to be given preferential treatment in India. Draft this document for the company's chairman.

2. Summarize the section of the topic concerning the Coca Cola company's dispute with the Indian government. This begins on line 20 and ends on line 61.
Write your summary using 60–70 words.

The Japanese Approach to Business

Preparation

1. What image do you have of the Japanese business executive?
2. What reasons can you think of for Japan's success in overseas markets?
3. Can you suggest some differences in management techniques or personnel policies between Japanese and Western companies?

Japan's invasion of Western markets has received widespread publicity in recent years. The success of its trading companies has indeed been spectacular. Not only have they held their ground in traditional markets but they have also conquered new fields formerly
5 dominated by powerful competitors. As one might expect, their activities have been viewed internationally with a mixture of admiration, envy and fear. Working on the principle that 'if you can't beat them, join them', the Western business community has begun to study closely how the Japanese system works. This examination has
10 revealed four elements which seem to create special attitudes and relationships in Japanese companies. We discuss these 'pillars' of the system below.

In most large companies, a policy of lifetime employment is practised. What this means is that when people leave school or
15 university to join an enterprise, they can expect to remain with that organization until they retire (usually at the age of 55 or 60). In effect, the employee gets job security for life, and can only be fired for serious misconduct. Even in times of business recession, he or she is free from the fear of being laid off or made redundant.
20 One result of this practice is that the Japanese worker identifies closely with his company and feels intense loyalty to it. By working hard for the company, he believes he is safeguarding his own future. It is not surprising that devotion to one's company is considered a great virtue in Japan. A man is often prepared to put his firm's
25 interests before those of his immediate family.

The job security guaranteed by this system influences the way employees approach their work. They tend to think in terms of what they can achieve throughout their career. This is because they are not judged on how they are performing during a short period of time,
30 perhaps when they are under pressure to increase company earnings. They can afford to take a longer perspective than their Western counterparts.

This marriage between the employee and the company — the consequence of lifetime employment — may explain why Japanese
35 workers seem positively to love the products their company is producing and why they are willing to stay on after work, for little overtime pay, to participate in earnest discussions about the quality control of their products.

Some people have criticized the principle of lifetime employment.
40 They point out that it works well in periods of boom, but when a

A happy employee of a big Japanese company. The company gives him a good salary, provided his flat at a low rent, and after advising him to get married, even introduced him to the girl he was attracted to!

recession comes, it can lead to rigidity and overmanning in companies. When the going gets tough, Japanese companies use various expedients to maintain the work force intact. For example, they may get rid of part-time workers first or perhaps keep workers
45 busy by transferring them to projects which will improve the future efficiency of the business. Nevertheless, if there is a prolonged slump, some of the methods can throw a strain on resources. Although common in large companies, lifetime employment is less prevalent in smaller companies. Also, while it applies to almost all
50 white-collar workers, fewer blue-collar ones get this kind of protection. Consequently, the blue-collar group shows greater job mobility.

Promotion by seniority is the next pillar of the system we shall look at. This policy means, first of all, that the more important and
55 responsible positions generally go to long-serving employees. For this reason, a young managing director is scarcely conceivable in Japan. It can take anything from 10 to 16 years for someone to reach even a middle-management post. Such a person is likely to be between 45 and 55 years old before reaching the level of department
60 manager. Secondly, salary levels are geared to years of service rather than to the responsibility of the job. The longer a person has been in a company, the higher his salary and status will probably be. Therefore, if two employees have joined the company at the same time, then ten years later, they will earn similar salaries even though
65 their responsibilities in the company may be different.

Because of this policy regarding salaries and promotion, employees will usually take on any work within their capacity; they do not object to training for new duties within the company since their salaries and fringe benefits will not be greatly affected. For the same reason, they are unlikely to resist technical change.

A final point is worth making. It is certain that an increasing number of young Japanese would like to be able to change their jobs without losing seniority, pay and other benefits. However, there is no great pressure to change to a system in which salaries would be strictly linked to ability and job responsibility.

Lastly, we turn to the consensus method of arriving at decisions in Japanese enterprises. Their term for this is *ringi seido* which can be translated as *consultation system*. The essence of the technique is that many employees at different management levels participate in the process of making decisions.

A second feature of the *ringi* system is that decisions evolve first from lower level management. They are not handed down from the top as in Western companies. This method is sometimes called 'bottom-up decision making'.

Here is an example of how the system works. A junior executive in a trading company may draft a report recommending some course of action. This document is then passed to the deputy head of the department. He will annotate it, perhaps even revise it, then stamp it with his personal seal (the equivalent of initialling). Before the report goes up to higher management, all the relevant departments of middle management will examine it, and after discussions, make their own modifications. From this, it can be seen that acceptance of a course of action does not depend essentially on approval being given at a particular level in a company. The plan will be approved in a prescribed form, in sequence, at various executive levels.

The *ringi* system may take as long as six months if a major proposal has been made, and because of this, it has been criticized as being a

A Quality Control Circle, ironing out problems and trying to increase productivity. These sessions take place after work, and are entirely voluntary with only a modest reward for participants.

slow and cumbersome method. Also, some say the process makes it
difficult to pin-point responsibility for mistakes. The Japanese argue,
100 however, that a lot of seals give a sense of security to the parties
concerned.

Decision-making through consensus creates what the Japanese call
wa. The word means 'harmony'. They believe that *wa* is essential in
any company or group. They contend that it is the group orientation
105 of managers, their teamwork and harmonious personal relations
which give companies their strength and efficiency.

The company union structure is the final pillar in the system. An
employee's union is based on the enterprise in which he works, not
on a national basis or by skills. All employees below section head are
110 eligible for membership, and it is quite common for union officials to
'cross the line' and become managers. Wage increases are generally
linked to the results of negotiations between national employers and
the union federations. These are settled at what is known as the
annual 'Spring labour offensive'.

115 Relations between unions and management tend to be rather cosy.
Serious labour disputes are rare. Take, for example, the Nissan
company which makes Datsun cars. Its plants in Japan have not had a
stoppage, let alone a strike, for over 20 years; nor for that matter have
its component suppliers had any production delays resulting from
120 industrial action during the same period.

Language Notes

Line 3	*Not only have they held their ground . . .* : Note how the normal word order changes when starting a sentence with *not only*. For example we can say either: a) He drinks heavily and he smokes. b) Not only does he drink heavily but he also smokes.
Line 5	*Competitor*: verb *compete*. One company competes with or against another company. Businessmen often complain of tough/acute/keen competition from rival firms.
Line 15	*University*. It is easy to make mistakes when using this word. Note these examples: I want to go to university. (No article) I am at university now. (No article) I am going to the University of Sussex. I am going to Sussex University. I graduated from the University of Sussex. (*Not* I was graduated from)
Line 17	*Fired*: dismissed or sacked. In colloquial English, a person might say he was *kicked out* or *thrown out* of a company.
Line 42	*When the going gets tough*: when conditions are unfavourable for business.
Line 47	*Slump*: a period when business activity decreases sharply. The opposite would be a *boom*.
Line 69	*Fringe benefits*: the term applies to certain benefits given to employees by the company, e.g. cost-price

purchases, use of a company car, subsidized lunches, Christmas bonuses. Another word with the same meaning is 'perks'.

A Comprehension

1. Describe some of the benefits which the practice of lifetime employment gives to the Japanese worker.
2. In a time of recession or slump, why is a Western company more flexible than a Japanese one?
3. Summarize the different approaches to salaries and promotion in Japanese and Western companies.
4. Why is the consensus method of arriving at decisions a democratic process?
5. Industrial relations in Japanese companies are usually good. Can you suggest reasons for this?

B Vocabulary

1. Find an appropriate word for each blank space. Initial letters are provided as clues to the correct answers.

   a) An advantage of the lifetime employment system is that workers enjoy a great deal of job s...... When business conditions are bad, they will not be made r...... Also, they will probably never be f...... unless they commit a serious offence. It should be noted that not all employees are protected by the system. Most w...... c...... workers are, but not all b...... c...... ones.

   b) A Japanese employee transferred to a less demanding position does not necessarily suffer a drop in salary or lose certain f...... b...... to which he was previously entitled. His earnings are usually g...... to the length of time he has been with the company. The Japanese approve of this system. However, they do not like the slow rate of promotion. A person usually does not reach a m......-m...... position before the age of 40 or 45.

   c) Consensus management means that many executives p...... in making decisions. Also, courses of action are often initiated at lower levels of management, for example by j...... e...... . The last person to be consulted in this process is sometimes the m...... d...... of the company.

2. Complete each sentence using an appropriate form of the word in *italics*.

   a) *publicity*   The problems of Europe's steel industries have been well ...... lately.

   b) *competition*   Some Western firms have found that they cannot ...... with Far Eastern manufacturers.

   c) *envy*   Many nations look ...... at the riches of oil-producing countries.

d) *loyal*   A dissatisfied employee may be ...... to the company he works for by divulging its secret processes or inventions to rival companies.

e) *influence*   The Marketing Manager is generally an ...... person in a company which sells consumer goods.

f) *criticize*   Once a major ...... of our product designs, he now admires them.

g) *efficient*   Someone with no interest in his job is likely to be ...... and unsatisfactory as a worker.

h) *responsible*   To work faster, some workers have been known to take the safety guard off their machines. This is a rather ...... act.

i) *likely*   There is little ...... that the Japanese will radically change their management techniques.

j) *object*   Some major ...... to the new highway scheme led to it being cancelled.

k) *decision*   A good manager needs to be fairly ....

l) *annotate*   My boss handed me an ...... version of the original report.

3. Circle the number next to the most suitable answer.

a) *If you can't beat them, join them* (l.7) is used in the text to imply that:
   (i) Western companies will soon have to give up competing with Japanese ones.
   (ii) Western businessmen are thinking of becoming partners in Japanese enterprises.
   (iii) Western companies will consider practising certain Japanese business methods.

b) The *longer perspective* of Japanese workers (l.31) refers to:
   (i) the attitude they can take to their work.
   (ii) the way they should be judged.
   (iii) the approach they take to company earnings.

c) An example of a *fringe benefit* (l.69) would be:
   (i) a promotion to a more highly paid position in the company.
   (ii) a substantial increase in an employee's annual salary.
   (iii) an interest-free loan made to the employee by the company.

d) *Pin-pointing responsibility for mistakes* (l.99) enables a company:
   (i) to improve labour-management relations significantly.
   (ii) to know precisely who has not done his job properly.
   (iii) to select staff who will not make a lot of mistakes.

e) The *Spring labour offensive* (l.114) refers to the time when:
   (i) employers take on large numbers of additional workers.
   (ii) many unions engage in negotiations for pay increases.
   (iii) the unions try to settle their differences with their employers.

C Language Practice

1. Supply the appropriate preposition for each blank space.

Example: *Result*
      (i) This action resulted *in* my dismissal.
      (ii) A fire resulted *from* the worker's carelessness.
      (iii) *As* a result of my work, I was promoted.

a) *view*
    (i) The Chairman viewed the group's pre-tax profits ...... pleasure.
    (ii) ...... view ...... their price increases, we shall not buy any more of their products.
    (iii) ...... the point of view of the consumer, price controls can be highly desirable.
    (iv) The tax changes are viewed ...... many people as being unnecessary
    (v) The company bought the freehold of the land ...... a view ...... extending the factory.

b) *business*
    (i) We are going to Kuwait ...... business.
    (ii) At present, many people want to do business ...... the Arabs.
    (iii) My friend is ...... business ...... his father-in-law. They operate a 'fast-food' restaurant.

c) *pressure*
    (i) The board members are putting pressure ...... the chairman to resign.
    (ii) A good manager should be able to work ...... pressure.

d) *criticize*
    (i) Our union has been criticized ...... acting against the company's interests.
    (ii) I am critical ...... many of the government's actions.
    (iii) We have been outspoken ...... our criticism ...... the decision to close down the plant.

e) *capacity*
    (i) We all admire his capacity ...... hard work.
    (ii) Because demand for our products has dropped, the factory is working ...... capacity.
    (iii) We are not sure what the capacity ...... the tank is.

f) *increase*
    (i) Our exports to the US increased ...... over 20% last year.
    (ii) We can increase our production ...... 10,000 units ...... 20,000 units per month.
    (iii) An increase ...... raw material costs could be disastrous for many building firms.

g) *relation*
    (i) It is difficult to judge our performance ...... relation ...... that of our biggest competitor.
    (ii) The trade relations ...... Japan and the West have been rather strained lately.

2. Complete the sentence openings to make meaningful sentences.

    a) *Not only does my secretary ......*

    b) *The longer I stay with this company, ...*

    c) *I'm sorry. I can't lend you 100 dollars, let alone ......*

    d) *It is not worth ......*

D Oral Work

1. Discussion Topics

    a) A Japanese professor[1] has written:
    'Confucianism, which is understood in Japan as an ethic rather than a religion, regards the following as most important:
     (i) Loyalty to the State or the Emperor
    (ii) Filial piety
    (iii) Faith in friendship
    (iv) Respect for seniors
    Confucianism is concerned with the relationship of one man to another or to the community to which he belongs; it is hardly concerned with the assessment of individual conduct or behaviour in itself, according to some absolute principles. So, in the Confucian world, individualism is suffocated.'
    Bearing in mind that most Japanese may be 'consciously or unconsciously regulated by Confucianism in their everyday conduct', comment on Japan's commercial success in the light of the remarks quoted above.

    b) The Japanese base salaries and promotion on the seniority of the employee in the company. What are your views on this system?

2. Argue for or against this debating theme:

    'Other countries should copy the Japanese system of setting up unions on a company basis.'

E Writing Exercises

1. The editor of a US business magazine with an international readership has just phoned. He wants you to write a short article entitled: 'Management, Japanese style'. During your conversation, he emphasized these two points:
    — the article should be a critical analysis.
    — readers would want to know the writer's personal views on the subject.
Write a draft of the article. Give comparisons with practices in your own country, where appropriate.

2. Summarize the section of the topic concerning lifetime employment. This begins on l.13 and ends on l.52.
Write your summary using 80–100 words.

1. Michio Morishima, Professor of Economics at the London School of Economics since 1970.

Everybody Loves a Winner — or do they?

Preparation

1. Which countries have most felt the effects of Japanese competition?
2. What different approaches have been used by governments to deal with the problem of Japanese imports?
3. Why is 'protectionism' generally undesirable? In what circumstances can it be justified?

He drives a Datsun, his son buzzes around on a Honda motorcycle. His wife listens to music on a Sony radio while she does the housework. He wears a Seiko watch and when he goes on holiday a Nikon camera is slung over his shoulder. His daughter wants to be a concert pianist; she practises daily on a Yamaha piano. Question: Who is he? Answer: A European.

The brand names mentioned above, all household words, bear witness to the invasion by Japanese exporters of European and North American markets during the 1970s. The Japanese have been efficient
10 in their business methods. They have made things people want to buy and they have marketed their goods aggressively. Their prices have been keen, their delivery dates firm. They have never been afraid to make initial losses in order to get a foothold in a new market.

15 Because of Japan's spectacular success, European and US manufacturers have found their own market shares, both domestic and overseas, diminishing drastically. Japanese competition has been exceptionally intense in basic industries such as steel and shipbuilding, but also in the car, motorcycle, consumer electronics
20 (especially TV sets and tubes) and ball-bearing industries. To give one example: in the first nine months of 1976, 86% of all new ship orders went to Japanese companies; or, to take another example, imagine the disappointment of the average German, whose country produces the Volkswagen car, when he learnt that in 1977, the three
25 top selling cars in the US were Japanese: the Toyota, Nissan (Datsun) and Honda respectively.

As pressure on European and US markets increased, trade officials and businessmen in the countries concerned began to react. Trade ministers in these areas drew attention to the huge trade surplus that
30 Japan had with the EEC and with the US. They stated that trade was clearly very one-sided and that Japan was not an open market for European exporters. On a trip to Japan, the British Trade Minister pointed out that Japan had an unnaturally low ratio of manufactures in its total imports: 20% instead of 50%.

35 The Japanese were also reproached for concentrating their export efforts in vulnerable European markets — the exporting companies concerned were said to receive powerful government support — and thus undermining European competitors in these sectors. The allegation was that they flooded these markets with cheap exports. In

40　some cases, companies were accused of dumping, i.e. selling abroad at lower prices than in the domestic market. The Japanese ball-bearing industry, for instance, was said, perhaps justifiably, to be selling products at 25% to 40% below domestic prices, and the EEC threatened to put a 15% tariff on bearing imports.

45　A constant source of irritation, according to European and US manufacturers, were the non-tariff barriers erected by Japan against imports. Japanese bureaucracy and red tape were often mentioned. There were often long delays, from four months to two years, in getting documents of approval for a new product to enter Japan and

50　delays in getting trade marks registered. A firm selling baby products said it could take months to get approval for a container or label change. The General Manager of the California Grape Commission recalled that 'Some inspectors took offence at the ink on the paper in which some grapes were wrapped. The ink had some fluorescence to

55　it. We had to dump the whole load in the sea.' Other grievances focused on the tough emission tests applied to car imports for environmental reasons.

Exporters were also not impressed by the expensive and complex distribution system in Japan. Too many middle-men were involved

60　before the goods reached retail outlets. These outlets were often located in narrow, inaccessible streets, which made distribution expensive. Such costs could add as much as 45% to a retail item. Coupled with higher production overheads, they could make foreign goods very expensive.

65　The Japanese reacted swiftly to these attacks although the steps they took sometimes created other problems. They agreed to exercise

The Robot Line. It turned out 20,000 Datsun car bodies a month with the aid of only 100 men. 96 per cent of the 2,700 welds are carried out by machine.

self-restraint by limiting steel exports to Europe, but then they increased their sales efforts in the US, with the result that US steel manufacturers started crying out for protection of their industry; no

70 sooner had Japanese companies agreed to limit car sales in Britain — a vulnerable market — than they began intensifying their sales drive in other European countries, causing concern to car manufacturers in these areas. Another of Japan's concessions was to raise ship-building prices and restrain exports, limiting their share of the

75 world market to about 50% instead of a potential 70%.

Other conciliatory gestures included: sending buying missions to Europe to look for likely imports such as car components whose prices were competitive with Japanese products; agreeing to send over inspectors to test cars and pharmaceuticals in the EEC countries

80 themselves rather than turning such products away at the dockside once they had arrived in Japan; investigating the possibility of setting up plants in Europe which would create employment and earn foreign currency for the countries concerned. In short, the Japanese bent over backwards to show that they were sensitive to the problems

85 caused in Europe and the US by their export successes.

While Japan has had brilliant and well-deserved achievements in its overseas trade, it would do well to heed warnings that have been delivered from expert sources. The first came from the world famous Hudson Institute which specializes in making long-term forecasts of a

90 country's economic prospects. In a study of Japan's trading future, it cautioned that the country lacked 'a natural trading region of high income nations where it could sell without provoking protectionist reactions.' Also, the country's growth was concentrated in areas which the Japanese would ultimately have to concede to lower wage

95 cost competitors, for example, South Korea, Taiwan and India.

Finally, the Director of International Economic Affairs at Keidenren stated that the current structure of Japanese trade had to be changed. His view was that 'The Japanese have put too much emphasis on developing basic heavy industries like steel and petrochemicals and

100 must shift to more knowledge-intensive industries like computers and systems for plant and equipment where the value-added factor is high'.

What is certain is that Japan must pay a huge bill for imports of food and raw materials. To do this, it relies heavily on the production

105 and export of manufactured goods, and these must be sold in countries with relatively high per capita incomes. It is doubtful, therefore, that Japan can change significantly the pattern of its trade in the short run.

Language Notes

Line 35	*Reproached for*: note also, blamed *for*, criticized *for*.
Line 36	*The exporting companies ...... were said to receive*: one could also say, 'It was said that they received'.
Line 44	*To put a tariff on*: a tariff is *put*, *imposed* or *levied* on goods.
Line 56	*Tough emission tests*. The Japanese authorities are very pollution-conscious. Car engines are tested to determine the volume, density and toxicity of the fumes they emit.
Line 69	*Crying out for*: demanding loudly and publicly.
Line 69	*No sooner ...... than*: note 'than' not 'that'.
Line 87	*To heed warnings*: to pay attention to. We also say: 'I shall heed his advice'.
Line 106	*Per capita incomes*: incomes per head or per person.

A Comprehension

1. What information in the text emphatically illustrates Japan's export success?
2. What are some of the criticisms made by Europeans of Japan's exporting strategy?
3. Foreign companies have often condemned the Japanese bureaucracy. Why?
4. What do the Japanese mean when they talk of 'self-restraint'? Why has this policy not always been popular with their competitors?
5. In what ways has Japan proved it is sensitive to the problems of foreign exporters?
6. The writer of this article hints that Japan may face problems in the years ahead. Specify the nature of these problems.

B Vocabulary

1. Find words or phrases in the text which mean the following:

Lines 8–34

Example: Name given by a manufacturer to one of their products.
— *Brand name*

a) Products known to most consumers.

b) To be proof of *or*
To testify to.

c) Competitive.

d) Unchanging.

e) To break into.

f) Percentage of total business available which is obtained by a company.

g) Excess of exports over imports.

h) Unfair, to the advantage of a particular country.

i) Country without trade restrictions.

Lines 35–64

    j) Blamed.

    k) Weak.

    l) Accusation.

    m) Sell in huge quantities.

    n) Complaints.

    o) Intermediaries.

    p) Places where goods are sold directly to the public.

2. Read the passage, then choose words or phrases from the box on the left to fill the blanks in the text.

> groupings
> sectors
> trade cycle
> innovation
> priority
> high-technology
> middle-management
> systematically
> nucleus
> core
> conglomerate
> marketable
> knowhow
> technical change

Why is Japan so successful in selling sophisticated, ... products in world markets? One obvious reason is that Japanese companies give ...... to research and development, and to technological .... Manpower and money is devoted to it on a continuous basis, regardless of the company's level of profitability at a particular time in the ....

Japanese companies also have a great ability to absorb .... Their unions do not oppose new technology; they welcome it and co-operate in introducing it into the company.

Many observers have noted that their companies search ...... throughout the world for the latest .... They are determined to be up-to-date in the technical field.

The Research and Development effort of these companies is highly organized. They have teams working on product possibilities, and they concentrate especially on ...... inventions.

The companies have been helped by the availability of large numbers of technical graduates able to do ...... jobs.

Finally, the Japanese effort has been based on powerful ...... of companies. The Japanese ...... is a type of organization not easily found in other countries. It consists of a hard ......: a trading company, a bank, and an insurance company; allied to that are manufacturing ......: engineering, shipbuilding, steel, real estate, etc. This all forms an enormous grouping round a central ....

3. Explain the meaning of these words or phrases within the text:

    a) Unnaturally low ratio of manufactures (l.33)

    b) Focused on (l.56)

    c) Inaccessible streets (l.61)

    d) Self-restraint (l.67)

    e) Conciliatory gestures (l.76)

    f) Bent over backwards (l.84)

    g) Knowledge-intensive industries (l.100)

C Language Practice

1. Write other sentences which are equivalent in meaning to the ones below. Use the sentence openings provided.

   a) It is essential for employees to work together harmoniously if an efficient, dynamic enterprise is to be created.
   Only by ......

   b) Imagine the disappointment of a West German when he hears that Datsun are outselling Volkswagen in the US.
   Think how ......

   c) The Japanese were reproached for concentrating their efforts in vulnerable US markets.
   A criticism ......

   d) There were often long delays in getting documents of approval for new products.
   To get documents of approval ......

   e) Distribution costs could add as much as 45% to a retail item.
   The price of a retail item ......

   f) US companies demanded protection when the Japanese increased their sales efforts.
   Japan's increased sales efforts led ......

2. Complete these sentences by supplying the appropriate preposition for each blank space.

   a) Japan's huge trade surplus ...... Britain shows the difficulties British exporters have experienced ...... selling to Japan compared ...... Japanese exporters selling in this country.

   b) Close links have been created ...... British and Japanese industries. ...... a result, the Japanese have showed increasing sensitivity ...... the problems ...... British industry.

   c) The Japanese market calls ...... high standards of quality and reliability, and its language and customs are unfamiliar ...... many exporters; ...... the other hand, foreign companies can claim that non-tariff barriers have hampered their efforts.

   d) The biggest obstacle ...... imports may be the traditional self-sufficiency of the Japanese. This creates a special attitude ...... imports.

   e) Westerners sometimes argue that Japan concentrates ...... applied development ...... the expense ...... basic research.

   f) The relations ...... the banks and industry in Britain have not always been conducive ...... success in export markets.

D Oral Work

1. Argue for or against the following debating theme:
   'If a wave of protectionism blows up in the US and Europe, the Japanese will only have themselves to blame.'

2. Role Play

The British Secretary of State for Trade (Trade Minister) has agreed to meet representatives of Datsun garages operating in Britain. The owners of these fear import controls will be placed on Datsun cars entering Britain. They recently wrote to the Minister saying: 'Our livelihood, the jobs of our employees, and those of many thousands of other workers employed producing components and spare parts for us are threatened by the long and persistent campaign regarding our car imports from Japan.'

The Minister is prepared to listen to what the garage owners have to say, but he will make it clear that the British car market cannot be 'flooded' by Japanese cars. He will also remind them of the huge amount of money the government has invested in British Leyland, the country's foremost car manufacturer. At this meeting, the Minister will be supported by a Junior Minister and a Treasury official.

Also invited to the discussion are the Japanese Minister for External Affairs and the Commercial Attaché to the Japanese in London.

Instructions

Students should be divided into three groups:

a) Representatives of Datsun garages in Britain;

b) The Secretary for State for Trade and his team;

c) The two invited Japanese officials.

The meeting will be chaired by the Secretary of State.

Enact the discussion.

3. Discussion Topic

Why is 'dumping' unfair? What reasons do countries have for dumping goods? What should other countries do when they suspect they are victims of this practice?

E Writing Exercises

1. Following the meeting between the British Secretary of State for Trade and representatives of the garage owners (see role-playing exercise), it was agreed by both sides that a statement should be made to the British press concerning the discussion that had taken place. The statement would be read out and circulated at a press conference to be held later that afternoon.
Working together in small groups (two or three members), students should draft versions of the press statement. The most satisfactory of these should be selected by the group as a whole for presentation at the press conference.

2. Discuss the impact Japanese exports have had on your country's economy. What are the attitudes of your government and the general public towards Japan's commercial performance in your own domestic market, and in overseas markets generally?

Bribery — an inevitable evil?

Preparation

1. Graft; payola; slush money; speed money (India); dash (Nigeria); shakedown. What do you think all these words and phrases have in common?
2. What kinds of bribes are offered in the business world? Can such payments be classified in any way?
3. Is bribery in business inevitable or can it be eliminated?

Students taking business courses are sometimes a little surprised to find that lectures on business ethics have been included in their syllabuses of study. They often do not realize that, later in their careers, they may be tempted to bend their principles to get what
5 they want; perhaps also they are not fully aware that bribery in various forms is on the increase in many countries, and, in some, this type of corruption has been a way of life for centuries.

    In dealing with the topic of business ethics, some lecturers ask students how they would act in the following situation: suppose you
10 were head of a major soft-drinks company and you want to break into a certain overseas market where the growth potential for your company is likely to be very great indeed. During negotiations with government officials of this country, the Minister of Trade makes it clear to you that if you offer him a substantial bribe, you will find it
15 much easier to get an import licence for your goods, and you are also likely to avoid 'bureaucratic delays', as he puts it. Now, the question is: do you pay up or stand by your principles?

    It is easy to talk about having high moral standards, but, in practice, what would one really do in such a situation? Some time ago
20 the British car manufacturer, British Leyland, was accused of operating a 'slush fund', and of other questionable practices such as paying agents and purchasers with padded commissions, offering additional discounts and making payments to numbered bank accounts in Switzerland. The company rejected these allegations and
25 they were later withdrawn. Nevertheless, at this time, there were people in the motor industry in Britain who were prepared to say in private: 'Look, we're in a wheeling-dealing business. Every year we're selling more than a £1,000 million worth of cars abroad. If we spend a few million greasing the palms of some of the buyers, who's
30 hurt? If we didn't do it, someone else would'.

    It is difficult to resist the impression that bribery and other questionable payments are on the increase. Indeed, they seem to have become a fact of commercial life. To take just one example, the Chrysler Corporation, third largest of the US motor manufacturers,
35 disclosed that it made questionable payments of more than $2.5 million between 1971 and 1976. By making this revelation, it joined more than 300 US companies who had admitted to the US Securities and Exchange Commission that they had made dubious payments of one kind or another — bribes, facilitating payments, extra discounts,

40 etc. — in recent years. For discussion purposes, we can divide these payments into three broad categories.

The first category consists of substantial payments made for political purposes or to secure major contracts. For example, the US conglomerate ITT (International Telephone and Telegraph

45 Corporation) offered a large sum of money in support of a US presidential candidate at a time when it was under investigation for possible violations of the US anti-trust law. This same company, it was revealed, was ready to finance efforts to overthrow the Marxist government of Chile whose President was Salvadore Allende.

50 In this category, we may also include large payments made to ruling families or their close advisers in order to secure arms sales or major petrochemical and construction contracts. In a court case involving an arms deal with Iran, a witness claimed that £1 million had been paid by a British company to a 'go-between' who helped

55 clinch a deal for the supply of tanks to that country. Other countries have also been known to put pressure on foreign companies to make donations to party funds.

The second category covers payments made to obtain quicker official approval of some project; to speed up the wheels of

60 bureaucracy. An interesting example of this kind of payment is provided by the story of a sales manager who had been trying for some months to sell road machinery to the Minister of Works of a Caribbean country. Finally, he hit upon the answer. Discovering that the minister was a bibliophile, he bought a rare edition of a book,

65 slipped $20,000 within its pages, then presented it to the minister. This man examined its contents, then said: 'I understand there is a two-volume edition of this work.' The sales manager, who was quick-witted, replied: 'My company cannot afford a two-volume edition, sir, but we could offer you a copy with an appendix!' A short

70 time later, the deal was approved.

The third category involves payments made in countries where it is traditional to pay people to facilitate the passage of a business deal. Some Middle East countries would be included on this list, as well as certain Far Eastern countries.

75 The payment may be made by a foreign company to ensure a tender is put on a selective contract list or the company may pay so that an import licence for essential equipment is approved. Sometimes an expensive gift may be necessary to soften up a government official.

80 A common type in this category is the 'facilitating payment' — usually a smaller sum of money — made to certain customs officials to clear cargoes. One businessman has told the story of a delivery of 10,000 bottles of sterile penicillin at the airport of a Far Eastern country. It was apparently customary to pay customs officials about

85 $250 upon arrival of each shipment to 'get them out of the sun'. In this case, the company was not prepared to make such a payment, so no money changed hands. The Minister of Health of that nation then ordered that each phial be opened for inspection, thereby destroying the whole shipment.

90 Is it possible to formulate a code of rules for companies which would outlaw bribery in all its forms? The International Chambers of Commerce (ICC) favours a code of conduct which would ban the giving and seeking of bribes. This code would try to distinguish

between commissions paid for real services and padded fees. A   *extra*
95   council has been proposed to administer the code.

Unfortunately, opinions differ among members of the ICC concerning how to enforce the code. The British members, led by Lord Shawcross, would like the system to have enough legal teeth to make companies behave themselves. 'It's no using having a dog
100   without teeth', they <u>argue</u>. However, the French delegates think it is   *reason*
the business of governments to make and impose law; the job of a business community like the ICC is to say what is right and wrong, but not to impose anything.

In a well-known British newspaper, a writer argued recently that
105   'industry is caught in a web of bribery' and that everyone is 'on the take'. This is probably an <u>exaggeration</u>. However, today's   *over estimation*
businessman, selling in overseas markets, will frequently meet situations where it is difficult to <u>square</u> his business interests with   *reconcile*
his moral conscience.

Language Notes

Line 1	*Taking business courses*: a person *takes*, *follows* or *goes on* a course of study.
Line 10	*Break into a market*: one could also say *get a foothold in*.
Line 17	*Stand by your principles*: stick to or maintain your high standards of behaviour.
Line 21	*Slush fund*: a fund used to make illegal or questionable payments. Slush is literally melting — often dirty — snow.
Line 22	*Padded commissions*: commissions which are in excess of the normal or 'going' rate.
Line 29	*Greasing the palms*: paying bribes.
Line 55	*Clinch a deal*: conclude a deal successfully.
Line 105	*On the take*: receiving bribes.
Line 108	*Square with*: reconcile; equate with.

A Comprehension

1. What purpose do lecturers have in asking students the question about the soft-drinks company?
2. What argument might someone in the British motor car industry use to justify the giving of bribes?
3. Why was the US company ITT criticized for making a large financial contribution to a political campaign?
4. The Minister of Works of the Caribbean country did eventually award the contract to the sales manager. What finally persuaded him to do this?
5. Explain briefly the difference of opinion existing within the International Chambers of Commerce about how the organization should deal with bribery.

B Vocabulary

1. Complete each group of sentences using an appropriate form of the word in *italics*.

   Ethics

   a) Giving a bribe to secure a contract would be considered ...... by an honest businessman.

   b) When working under pressure, someone might find it hard to do what is ...... correct.

   Corrupt

   a) ...... can in some countries become the normal ingredient of an aggressive sales policy.

   b) Some officials will under no circumstances accept bribes. They are ....

   c) He was charged with ...... accepting unauthorized payments.

   Moral

   a) It is easy to ...... when one has never been in a position to be tempted.

   b) She is a person of very high ....

   c) One must inevitably question the ...... of his action.

   d) To offer money for corrupt purposes is ....

   e) Having no sense of what is right or wrong, he is in fact totally ....

   Approve

   a) Securing official ...... for the import of goods can be costly in some countries.

   b) Tenders for contracts have to be submitted in the ...... form.

   c) Many authorities express public ...... of bribery, yet do little to try to stamp it out.

   d) The goods will be sent to you on ....

Tempt

a) To many people, the offer of a country house would be very
....

b) Most people experience the ...... to act against their principles.

Admit

a) It is, ..., difficult to know the right course to follow in certain
situations.

b) An ...... fact at his trial was that he had offered a bribe.

2. Supply any appropriate word for each blank space.
In many countries, it is common to pay someone to ease the
passage of a business .... For a company ...... into these markets
for the first time, the ...... to use bribery is very great indeed. In
many cases, the company will have to pay inflated ...... to an agent
or make other such payments if an order is to be .... Later, there
will be the routine handout to make sure the consignment of
goods is ...... through customs. Although an international
business community like the ICC can give guidelines to
companies, it cannot ...... bribery by its own efforts. It is up to
governments in those countries where bribery is ...... to help
stamp out this ...... by bringing in laws against corruption and
making sure these are ....

3. Circle the letter next to the most suitable interpretation.

a) Those who are tempted to bend their principles (l.4):
   (i) generally are people without any principles.
   (ii) usually change their principles according to
   circumstances.
   (iii) rather unwillingly make some kind of compromise.

b) If you are in a wheeling-dealing business (l.27), you should
expect:
   (i) to be involved in deals worth millions of pounds.
   (ii) to have frequent and extensive disputes with dealers.
   (iii) to work fast under pressure to get results.

c) Speeding up the wheels of bureaucracy (l.59) will probably:
   (i) reduce administrative delays for a company.
   (ii) involve many contacts with official machinery.
   (iii) mean greater interference by government officials.

d) When a tender is put on a selective contract list (l.76):
   (i) a company gains an advantage over some of its
   competitors.
   (ii) no other company is allowed to bid for the contract.
   (iii) a company is almost certain to be awarded the contract.

e) Industry is caught in a web of bribery (l.105). This statement
implies that:
   (i) bribery is widespread and difficult for a businessman to
   avoid.
   (ii) almost everyone in industry is engaged in taking bribes.
   (iii) anyone entering industry will almost certainly be
   corrupted.

C Language Practice

1. Make sentences from these notes.

   a) Argued; bribery; widespread; industry; many countries.

   b) Businessmen; used to; payments; customs officers; ensure; goods; rapidly.

   c) Many companies; USA; admitted; bribes; large contracts.

   d) Some governments; pressure; foreign companies; donations; political purposes.

   e) US company ITT; unsuccessful; attempt; finance; overthrow; Marxist regime; Chile.

   f) The International Chambers of Commerce; proposed; council; set up; administer; code.

2. Forming complex sentences: rewrite each of the following groups of sentences as **one** sentence. Do **not** use *and*, *but* or *because*. Make any other necessary changes.

   a) Many enterprises have to choose between giving in to extortion or not doing business. They are usually willing to pay bribes to stay in the market. This should surprise no one.

   b) Some Middle East governments are worried about their image abroad. They have decided to investigate the conduct of certain agents. The commissions of these agents are said to be excessive.

   c) The ICC recognizes that political contributions are usually legitimate. It also realizes that these may sometimes be used as bribes. It argues that governments should make laws to ensure such payments are recorded.

   d) Many people are pessimistic. The ICC is convinced bribery can be limited. Companies must be willing to disclose details of questionable payments they are asked to make.

3. Complete these sentences by supplying the appropriate prepositions.

   a) The ICC drew ...... a report in which it put ...... proposals to limit the growth of bribery.

   b) The report, while acknowledging it was impossible to stamp ...... the practice entirely, laid ...... certain principles of conduct for businesses.

   c) In the USA, people say that since the business community has failed to come .... its own code, the government should step ....

   d) The British, backed up ...... many other countries, were in favour of legal enforcement of the code; others could not go ...... with this idea. It is uncertain which side will eventually back ...... and offer some kind of compromise.

e) Some countries have brought ...... laws to limit bribery.

f) The ICC commission ran ...... many problems during its meetings. Its first draft code had to be watered ...... because some provisions were considered too tough.

D Oral Work

1. Argue for or against the following debating theme:

   'If one is to succeed in business, it is essential to learn the art of giving a bribe, therefore high principles and business success are incompatible.'

2. Role Play

   You are the Sales Director of an educational publishers. One of your firm's best-selling books is an English language course book giving the foreign student a thorough grounding in the elements of the language. This textbook is doing particularly well in Asian markets at present. Recently, you and your Managing Director went on an Asian sales tour, and in one of the countries you visited, the two of you met an official in the Ministry of Education. During the meeting, this man mentioned that it might be possible to get your textbook used throughout the country's secondary school system, but he hinted that he expected some sort of bribe from you for his co-operation.
   Instructions
   Working in groups of three, students should take roles and enact the discussion which took place between the Sales Manager, Managing Director and Ministry of Education official.

E Writing Exercises

1. Discuss some of the ways in which a business executive might have to compromise his personal ethics for the sake of his company's interests.

2. You are the chairman of a company, based in Birmingham, England, which markets cutlery in the UK and overseas. You have recently learned, to your surprise, that your sales department has been operating a 'slush fund'. From this fund, secret payments have been made to individuals setting up deals or who have, however indirectly, contributed to the winning of a contract. You are very upset to learn about the existence of this fund, especially since the frequency and size of such payments seem to have increased greatly in the last two years. Accordingly, you call your Marketing Manager, Mr Sherwood, to give him a piece of your mind and tell him that these questionable payments must cease immediately. To your surprise he does not agree with you . . .

   Write the dialogue that takes place between yourself, as Chairman, and the Marketing Manager.

Industrial Democracy in Britain

Preparation

1. How would you define the term 'industrial democracy'?
2. Is it desirable to have employee representatives (worker representatives) on the board of directors of a company? If so, why?
3. What could be some of the problems of having worker directors?

'Don't you say Bullock to me!'

'In our view, it is no longer acceptable for companies to be run on the basis that in the last resort the shareholders' view must by right always prevail.'

'Now is the time to provide for the growing and unused capacities of organized labour, by giving them representatives on the boards of large enterprises.'

Quotations from the *Bullock Report*

Industrial democracy is generally taken to mean that those who work in a business should share democratically in the responsibility for managing it; in other words, employees at every level in a company should share in the decisions which affect their working lives. In
5 Western countries, industrial democracy has generally been achieved by having workers represented on works councils or on boards of directors.

Many European countries (for example: West Germany, Sweden and Denmark) have for several years been practising some form of
10 worker participation in the management of enterprises. Britain, however, was late to get in on the act. It was in 1975 that the British government finally commissioned a report on this subject, and a Committee of Inquiry published its proposals in 1977.

The chairman of this committee was Lord Bullock, an Oxford
15 University historian and also Master of St Catherine's College, Oxford. His ten-man team consisted of academics, industrialists and trade union members. The committee's terms of reference were as follows:

'Accepting the need for a radical extension of industrial democracy
20 in the control of companies by means of representation on boards of directors, and accepting the essential role of trade union organizations in this process, to consider how such an extension can best be achieved . . .'

The series of proposals made by the committee covered seven
25 million workers: roughly one-third of the country's work-force. Here are some details about two important and controversial recommendations made in the report.

Board composition
The committee proposed that employee representatives should be
30 introduced on to company boards of management. For all British and foreign firms based in Britain with 2000 or more employees, there

should be *equal representation* of employees and shareholders, with a smaller group of co-opted directors. Thus, company boards would be composed of three elements:

35 1. Employees
    2. Shareholder representatives
    3. A smaller group of co-opted directors

This proposal became known as the 2X+Y board formula.

The third group would be selected by the other two groups, and 40 would form less than one-third of the total board. The idea of the co-opted directors was to allow persons with special experience and expertise to be brought into the boardroom from inside or outside the company. There might be someone among senior or middle-management whom both sides might wish to include, or 45 perhaps someone from outside the company; a solicitor, banker, accountant or national trade union official.

Choice of worker representatives

The committee proposed that employee representatives should be chosen by the unions and, in practice, it thought employees would 50 probably select shop stewards. These are union representatives actually working on the shop floor. For many workers, they are the first point of contact with the union structure.

A vital recommendation of the committee, therefore, was that worker representation should be based on the union machinery 55 within the company. Once employees of a company had decided — by means of a ballot — that they wanted employee representation, then the unions in that company should be allowed to devise an appropriate system of selecting worker representatives.

The Bullock proposals aroused great interest. They also came under 60 heavy fire, being criticized by government officials, the press, management and even by some trade unionists.

The powerful Confederation of British Industry (CBI), which represents British management, objected to union-nominated directors being imposed on boards. It was supported by the *Times* 65 newspaper who saw these proposals as 'a transfer of power to the unions'. The newspaper believed that workers had a right to be represented by whom they chose, and that, in this case, the rights of

The Bullock Committee. At the far end of the table is the Chairman, Lord Bullock, Master of St. Catherine's College, Oxford.

non-union workers, including managers, had been largely ignored.

Many people did not like the idea of parity of directors, the
70 fifty/fifty idea. They argued that, if this was adopted, the majority of
the board would be composed of people with little or no experience
of the executive problems of a company.

About a year later, the government produced a White Paper[1]
entitled *Industrial Democracy*. The proposals in it represented a
75 compromise with the ideas put forward by the Bullock committee.

The White Paper advocated that employees in companies with 500
or more workers should have a legal right to be consulted on all major
proposals of the company affecting them, before any decisions were
taken. Consultation would be effected by using Joint Representation
80 Councils composed of members of all the unions within a company.
Discussions would cover such matters as investment plans, mergers,
takeovers, major redundancies and organizational changes.

Finally, employees in companies with more than 2,000 workers
would have a legal right to appoint up to one-third of the directors on
85 the board of a company. Government finance would be made
available to train worker directors who would need a knowledge of
business finance, management and other subjects to be effective
board members.

1. A document published by the government containing proposals for new legislation. It is designed to provide the basis for discussion and constructive criticism.

" I'VE A FEELING WE'RE NOT WELCOME, BERT ! "

Language Notes

Line 11	*To get in on the act*: to show serious interest in the idea of worker participation in decision-making.
Line 12	*Commissioned*: used in the sense of 'entrusting a person or a group with a task to perform'.
Line 15	*Master*: a title given to some administrative heads of Oxford colleges.
Line 33	*Co-opted*: elected into a body by the votes of existing members.
Line 45	*Solicitor*: member of the legal profession. He or she advises clients and prepares cases for barristers. In Britain, solicitors do not generally appear as advocates, except in lower courts.
Line 56	*Ballot*: secret vote.

A Comprehension

1. What, in your view, is the meaning of the *first* quotation from the Bullock report that is given at the beginning of the text?
2. Some people criticized the selection of Alan Bullock as chairman of the Committee of Inquiry. Can you suggest why?
3. What do you understand by the phrase *terms of reference*?
4. Read again the terms of reference of the committee (l.19–23). In what sense did these *limit* the committee members in their inquiry?
5. The proposed board structure was known as the 2X+Y formula. What does the Y represent? Why was it included in the formula?
6. Suggest reasons why the majority of trade unionists welcomed the proposals of the committee.
7. What is the main difference between the Bullock Committee proposal and that of the White Paper concerning the composition of company boards?

B Vocabulary

1. Complete each sentence using an appropriate form of the word in *italics*.

   a) *democracy* Most unions insist that their officials should be ...... elected.

   b) *responsibility* Although young and inexperienced, she behaved very ...... in her new job.

   c) *represent* Our company have opted for equal ...... of workers and shareholders on our board.

   d) *control* That industrial group has a ...... interest in smaller enterprises.

   e) *director* A friend of mine holds ......s in over twenty companies.

f) *manage*   We have great talent in the ...... ranks of our organization.

g) *recommend*   New legislation will be along the lines ...... by the White Paper.

h) *shareholder*   I cannot tell you offhand the size of my ...... in that company.

i) *select*   We went to a rather ...... cocktail party last night.

j) *include*   Our sales team will stay at the hotel from the 10th to the 17th ....

k) *impose*   The ...... of equal representation would not have been well received by the Confederation of British Industry.

l) *adopt*   ...... of the Bullock proposals without modification could be disastrous.

m) *advocate*   ...... of the German approach to industrial democracy is becoming common.

n) *consult*   Since he works for a firm of engineering ......s, he travels frequently.

o) *plan*   A British company recently won a contract for the ...... and building of an entirely new city in Saudi Arabia.

2. Here is a statement by a government official. Read it, then choose words or phrases from the box on the left to fill the blanks in the text.

joint decision-making
crucial
dissent
committed
minority
chairmanship
unanimous
representation
co-opt
terms of reference
submitted
board level

The Committee of Inquiry, which came into being during December 1975, under the ...... of Lord Bullock, ... its report to me last month.

The report of the committee is not .... There is a majority report, signed by the Chairman and six members of the committee, but with a note of ...... by one of the six. There is also a ...... report signed by the remaining three members.

The majority of the committee recommended legislation to give employees the right to ...... on the boards of companies.

The reconstituted board would be composed of equal numbers of employee and shareholder representatives who would ...... a further small number of directors.

The minority report criticized the ...... of the committee, saying that they presupposed a commitment to employee representation on boards. I would like to make it clear that our government remains ...... to the ...... role of the trade unions in the process of extending industrial democracy.

It is the government's view that arrangements for ...... at all levels will make a major contribution to improved labour relations. The government would also like employees in nationalized industries to have the right to representation at ....

C Language Practice

1. In this exercise, you can read a selection of comments made at the time the Bullock committee report was published. Explain briefly what each italic word or phrase means.

    a) The Bullock report, a *blueprint* for board-room sharing, was published today.

    b) Publication of the report *triggered* a furious reaction from industrialists.

    c) There is a wide *rift of opinion* concerning the main proposals.

    d) The clash between the government and leading industrialists *came to a head* last night when the CBI asked for an urgent meeting with the Prime Minister.

    e) The formula of equal representation on boards of employees and shareholder representatives is a sure recipe for *stalemate*.

    f) The proposals would be unrepresentative since they would *disenfranchise* managers and other employees who were not members of trade unions.

    g) The proposals would *bring about* a revolution in Britain's *deeply-entrenched* attitudes towards industrial relations.

    h) My experience as an industrialist convinces me that participation must begin *at the grass roots*, on the shop floor and in the office.

    i) Lord Bullock was unavailable for comment since he was on holiday, *away from the limelight*.

    j) One must ask why the report has created such *a furore* in recent weeks.

    k) The question of employees' representation *has now been placed on the agenda of* British politics, and will not easily be removed.

    l) The violent criticism of the report has put the government *in a quandary*.

2. Supply an appropriate preposition for each blank space.

    a) The government is committed ...... introducing industrial democracy ...... the trade union machinery.

    b) The proposals would result ...... a shift of power ...... shareholders ...... company boards.

    c) The Bullock report marks such a giant leap ...... the unknown that everyone is fearful ...... its consequences.

    d) A company might receive a bid ...... its shares which was advantageous ...... shareholders but carried bad implications ...... labour.

    e) Reactions ...... the report have varied ...... complimentary ...... vitriolic.

f) Shareholders would be stripped ...... some traditional powers; some senior managers would become answerable ...... the men they control.

g) The banks and insurance companies are totally opposed ...... worker directors as envisaged ...... the Bullock committee.

h) As companies have grown ...... size and complexity, they have tended to become remote ...... the communities ...... which they operate.

i) Getting workers ...... all levels to identify themselves ...... the company ...... which they work is difficult.

j) The CBI condemned the report findings ...... moving too fast, discriminating ...... non-union labour, and having a disastrous effect ...... overseas confidence.

k) The committee recommends that trade unions should have the right to nominate their members ...... a process of their own choosing ...... the boards of companies.

l) An important proposal of the committee was that worker directorships would be established only ...... an application by a recognized trade union, and confirmed ...... a ballot of all employees.

D Oral Work

1. Argue for or against the following debating themes:

   a) 'Since it is the shareholders who provide the risk capital for most companies, it is they alone who should determine the composition of company boards.'

   b) 'Governments in industrialized countries should enact laws stating that a certain minimum percentage of board members must be women.'

2. Discussion Topics

   a) In the government's White Paper on Industrial Democracy, it was proposed that where companies would not accept worker directors voluntarily, the law would enforce new, two-tier boards with worker directors occupying a third of the seats on a policy-making Upper Board. This board would appoint a second 'Management Board' consisting of all the top executives and would also fix their salaries. The Management Board would carry out the day-to-day management of the company. These executives would be answerable to the policy board which would make all major decisions on strategy, finance, takeovers and mergers.

      To avoid being forced into a two-tier system, a firm would have to agree to give up one-third of the seats on its existing single (unitary) board to worker representatives.
      — What would you say are the advantages and disadvantages of this proposal?

3. Role Play

Shortly after publication of the Bullock committee's findings, the British Prime Minister agreed to meet representatives of various groups affected by the proposals. He hoped for a frank exchange of views although he realized the discussion might become heated. These persons were at the meeting:
— Prime Minister (chairman)
— Secretary of State for Trade
— Chairman of the Confederation of British Industry (CBI)
— Group of company directors
— Group of trade union officials
— Shareholder representatives

Here is the document circulated as an aide-mémoire for members.

THE MAIN PROPOSALS

1. Main boards of companies should consist of two groups representing workers and shareholders, with a smaller group co-opted.
2. If a union with bargaining rights for 20 per cent of employees requests it, a secret ballot should be held on having worker-directors.
3. If the decision is in favour, a joint committee of all unions should elect directors.
4. A training programme for the worker-directors should be set up — with £3 million of Government cash for the first three years.
5. An Industrial Democracy Commission should be set up to help start the system.

6. Worker-directors should not get fees, but would get time off and secretarial services.

The three dissenting committee members proposed in their minority report:
a) A two-tier system as in Germany with workers going only on a supervisory board, leaving the day-to-day running of companies in the hands of management.
b) Employee-directors should include at least one of every grade of employee — including management.
c) All employees — not just union members — should take part in elections.
d) Banks and insurance companies should be exempt.

Instructions: students should represent either individuals or group interests. The meeting should then be enacted with the Prime Minister in the chair.

E Writing Exercises

1. On the next page, you can read a number of reactions to the Bullock proposals and the White Paper which followed. The

language is informal and colloquial. You should transfer these comments into the more formal style of Reported Speech. An example is given to help you do the exercise.

Example:

'Look, I'm like everyone else. I think participation and joint-decision making, call it what you want, is fine. Just fine. If your company's any size at all, you've got to find a way of achieving it. But, for Heaven's sake, don't ask me to speak up for Bullock.'
(An industrialist)

An industrialist said that, like most of his colleagues, he was a strong supporter of employee participation. In companies of any size, it was essential that machinery existed for achieving it. However, he refused to support the Bullock committee's proposals.

a) 'I like it. In fact, I like it enormously. The White Paper is really on the right track. It's got rid of that ridiculous 50/50 board formula Bullock wanted to thrust down our throats. But I still think the White Paper should have played down the union angle more. Still, all in all, a nice piece of work by the Government — for once!'
(Industrial editor speaking on TV about the government White Paper)

b) 'I think it's all unfair. There's no way I want to belong to a union — can't stand them — so who's going to look after me? In any case, what's the use of putting a few of us blokes on the board. We wouldn't have a clue what to say. I'm a machine operator in a car factory. Nobody asks me anything, and if something's going on in the company, I usually hear about it from the tea-lady.'
(A factory worker)

c) 'Some first rate ideas in that report. Very sensible for worker directors to be selected by the unions. After all, we know the kind of person who'll stand up for us at board meetings . . . I must say, I don't like that bit about co-opted directors, but they'll drop that idea sooner or later. As for the minority report — a load of rubbish!'
(A trade union official)

d) 'The way I see it, those **!!**** committee members were trying to slip worker control on to boards without us realizing it. If I remember rightly, half of those members were trade unionists, weren't they?'
(A company director)

2. Discuss this view of industrial democracy:
'Industrial democracy in its widest sense, can only be fully achieved when all those working in industry have a real desire to see its implementation. If it is to be effective, it must begin at the grass roots, on the shop floor and in the office, rather than be imposed at the top level first.'

Swiss Banking Secrecy

Preparation

1. What kind of reputation do Swiss banks have internationally?
2. What are 'numbered accounts'? Why do people use them?
3. Should a government department be able to force a bank to disclose details of a depositor's financial transactions?

Since the early 1930s, Swiss banks had prided themselves on their system of banking secrecy and numbered accounts. Over the years, they had successfully withstood every challenge to this system by their own government who, in turn, had been frequently urged by
5 foreign governments to reveal information about the financial affairs of certain account holders. The result of this policy of secrecy was that a kind of mystique had grown up around Swiss banking. There was a widely-held belief that Switzerland was irresistible to wealthy foreigners, mainly because of its numbered accounts and bankers'
10 reluctance to ask awkward questions of depositors. Contributing to the mystique was the view, carefully propagated by the banks themselves, that if this secrecy was ever given up, foreigners would fall over themselves in the rush to withdraw money, and the Swiss banking system would virtually collapse overnight.
15 To many, therefore, it came like a bolt out of the blue, when, in the summer of 1977, the Swiss banks announced they had signed a five-year pact with the Swiss National Bank (the Central Bank). The aim of this agreement was to prevent the improper use of the country's bank secrecy laws, and its effect was to curb severely the
20 system of secrecy. A headline in a British newspaper at that time aptly summed up the general view: *Numbered accounts' days are numbered*.
The new code which the banks had agreed to observe made the opening of numbered accounts subject to much closer scrutiny than
25 before. The banks would be required, if necessary, to identify the origin of foreign funds going into numbered and other accounts. The idea was to stop such accounts being used for dubious purposes. Also, the banks agreed not to facilitate in any way capital transfers from countries which had introduced laws to restrict the transfer of
30 capital abroad. Finally, they agreed not knowingly to accept funds resulting from tax evasion or from crime.
The pact represented essentially a tightening up of banking rules. Although the banks agreed to end relations with clients whose identities were unclear or who were performing improper acts, they
35 were still not obliged to inform on a client to anyone, including the Swiss government. To some extent, therefore, the principle of secrecy had been maintained.
What eventually persuaded the banks to allow restrictions to be placed on their cherished system of secrecy and numbered accounts?

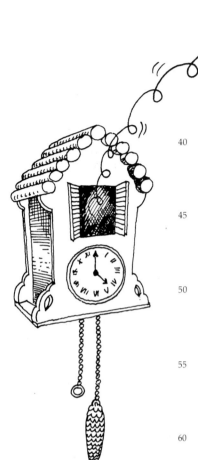

40 To answer this question, we will take a historical perspective and look back at events leading up to this significant change in banking policy.

The solid foundation of the system was provided by the Swiss bank secrecy law of 1934. This made it a penal offence to provide
45 information about a bank's clients without their explicit authorisation, unless a court ordered otherwise.

At that time, the law was designed to protect Jewish and other account holders in Germany against informers. The Nazi authorities had imposed stiff penalties, including capital punishment, for anyone
50 transferring money abroad, and they were in the habit of sending agents into Switzerland to track down the assets of German Jews and others intending to flee the Nazi regime. The Swiss Parliament placed banking secrecy under the protection of the law after a Gestapo agent seduced a young woman employee and obtained the identities of
55 some depositors.

Unfortunately, some banks began to abuse the protection afforded by this law. Critics both inside and outside the country, frequently accused them of irregular practices. Some said the banks were havens for smuggled currency and that they provided a shield for tax
60 evasion. A socialist Member of Parliament claimed that banking secrecy had helped Switzerland to become a *nation of receivers of stolen goods*. It was also believed that ransom money from a number of kidnappings in Italy was paid into Swiss banks in the southern Swiss canton of Ticino, located near the Swiss/Italian border.

65 About three years ago, the National Bank started talks with the Swiss Bankers' Association (85% of the commercial banks belong to this) to persuade the banks to be less tight-lipped about their operations and more forthcoming with information. It had to give up the attempt because the Association carried out a vigorous publicity
70 campaign, complaining that the mere rumour of less secrecy had already caused foreigners to withdraw funds.

What unquestionably pushed — some say stampeded — the Swiss banks into limiting secrecy was the huge financial scandal involving the Crédit Suisse: one of Switzerland's 'big three' banks. The
75 notoriety of the affair badly tarnished the Swiss banks' image of stability and honesty.

The scandal came to light when the Crédit Suisse bank revealed that the manager of one of its major branches in Chiasso, near the Italian border, had been involved in secret, unauthorized deals.
80 These had resulted in gigantic losses to the bank. Some estimated the eventual figure might reach £300 million or more.

The manager of the bank, Ernest Kuhrmeier, and an assistant, were said to have channelled about two billion dollars (£500 million) illegally into a Liechtenstein company, Texon Finanzanstalt. The

85 manager had a stake in this company. The money used had come into
the bank, over a fifteen-year period, from Italians who had hoarded
lire, then wanted to convert their currency into stronger Swiss francs.

Kuhrmeier had apparently offered these depositors Swiss credit
guarantees for their investments without telling Head Office, and
90 then he had got Texon to reinvest the money in Italian companies
dealing in plastics, wine and other such products. Most of these
enterprises had folded up.

When it became known in banking circles that Texon's investments
were disastrous, the Swiss banking community put pressure on
95 Crédit Suisse to make a clean breast of everything. Bankers feared
that confidence in the entire banking system would be undermined.
When the scandal was disclosed, it made headlines internationally.
Almost immediately, there followed a radical shake-up of the Crédit
Suisse organization, both at Chiasso and at head office where the
100 chief executive was replaced. The National Bank and two other major
commercial banks offered to lend Crédit Suisse the money to cover its
losses, but the bank turned down the offer. It was confident it could
cover all the Chiasso guarantees.

An important result of the Crédit Suisse fiasco was that the Swiss
105 banks were forced to tighten their rules and formalize their behaviour
regarding banking secrecy. As we have already mentioned, pressure
to reform the system had been building up for years. It needed this
debacle to tip the banks towards reform. The Swiss Director General
of the National Bank was undoubtedly right when he stated publicly
110 that Switzerland's status as a banking centre was based not on
numbered accounts, but on the social and economic stability of the
country.

Language Notes

Line 1	*Prided themselves on*: we pride ourselves *on* something. Note however: take pride *in* and be proud *of*.
Line 15	*A bolt out of the blue*: a great surprise or shock. A 'bolt' is literally a discharge of lightning. An alternative for this expression is: *It came as a bombshell* ......
Line 23	*The new code ...... agreed to observe*: people 'observe' or 'comply with' a code, rules, regulations etc.
Line 39	*Cherished system*: a system which the banks value highly.
Line 58	*Havens*: these are literally 'harbours' or 'places of refuge'.
Line 61	*Receivers of stolen goods*: people who buy stolen goods, then resell them. They are sometimes called 'fences'.
Line 72	*Stampeded*: a stampede occurs when a group of animals flee in panic for some reason, e.g. fire or the presence of other dangerous animals.
Line 75	*Notoriety*: fame, but in a bad sense.
Line 104	*Fiasco*: shameful episode or event.
Line 108	*Debacle*: similar in meaning to *fiasco*, a disastrous event.

A Comprehension

1. Why had the Swiss banks and the government frequently clashed over the years?
2. *Numbered accounts' days are numbered.* Explain the meaning of this headline published at the time of the pact.
3. Why could one say that the new code did not entirely destroy the banks' traditional system of secrecy?
4. Some people accused the banks of being 'havens for smuggled currency'. What exactly did they mean?
5. What protection did the 1934 Bank Secrecy Law give to customers of banks?
6. How did the manager of the Crédit Suisse bank in Chiasso finance his Liechtenstein company?
7. What costly mistake did that particular manager make?
8. What was the most important consequence of the Crédit Suisse scandal?

B Vocabulary

1. Explain the meaning of the expressions in *italics* which are either in the text or were used by people referring to the topic.

   a) If secrecy were lost, foreigners would *fall over themselves* to withdraw money.

   b) It came *like a bolt out of the blue* when the Swiss banks announced their pact.

   c) The National Bank asked the commercial banks to be less *tight-lipped* about their operations.

   d) The manager was said *to have a stake* in a Liechtenstein company.

   e) Most of the Italian companies *folded up*.

   f) When a banking scandal occurs, the bank concerned tries to *play down* its importance.

   g) People put pressure on Crédit Suisse to *make a clean breast of* everything.

   h) After the scandal, there was a *shake-up* of the Crédit Suisse organization.

   i) Some well-off Italians like to *salt away* money in neighbouring Switzerland.

   j) The banks were pushed into signing the pact *in the wake of* the Chiasso scandal.

2. Circle the number next to the most appropriate interpretation of the word in *italics*.

   a) The banks have *withstood* every challenge by the government.
   (i) refused   (ii) resisted   (iii) accepted

b) A *mystique* has grown up around Swiss banking.
   (i) atmosphere of lies   (iii) aura of secrecy
   (ii) air of disbelief

c) This view was *propagated* by the banks themselves.
   (i) spread   (ii) held   (iii) believed

d) The effect of the pact was to *curb* the system of secrecy.
   (i) destroy   (ii) improve   (iii) limit

e) People said the banks *provided a shield for tax evasion*. This means:
   (i) The banks were actively persuading people to avoid paying tax.
   (ii) The banks were accepting money on which tax should have been paid.
   (iii) The banks were making efforts to avoid paying their taxes.

f) What *stampeded the banks into* placing restrictions on secrecy was ......
   (i) made the banks act wisely
   (ii) made the banks act sensibly
   (iii) made the banks act hastily

g) The affair *tarnished* the banks' reputation of stability.
   (i) weakened   (ii) stained   (iii) ruined

h) Italians who had *hoarded* lire wanted to change their currency into Swiss francs.
   (i) invested   (ii) deposited   (iii) stored up

i) *It needed this debacle to tip the banks towards reform*. This sentence means:
   (i) The scandal made the banks change their policies very quickly.
   (ii) The scandal was necessary finally to persuade the banks to make changes
   (iii) The scandal immediately forced the banks to carry out reforms.

3. Complete the sentences using an appropriate form of the words in *italics*.

   a) *secrecy*   The Swiss banks have always been ...... about their operations.

   b) *withdraw*   After the scandal, some ...... of funds from Crédit Suisse was to be expected.

   c) *origin*   Most banking frauds ...... from bad surveillance of staff.

   d) *evasion*   If you ask a bank manager to lend you money, you may find him ...... the question!

   e) *penal*   All the other banks should not be ...... for the misbehaviour of one branch.

f) *habit*   People who ...... have overdrafts sometimes end up by becoming very rich!

g) *information*   This bank prospectus is most ......

h) *scandal*   Many Swiss people were ...... when news of the Chiasso affair reached them.

i) *convert*   Many currencies are not immediately ...... into dollars.

j) *guarantee*   When I bought my house, my father was ...... for some money I borrowed.

k) *confidence*   This bank reference is marked 'Private and ......'.

l) *commercial*   It is a pity when a small and beautiful seaside town becomes ......

C Language Practice

1. Make sentences from these notes.

    a) Many foreigners doubt/new agreement/change/Swiss banks/system/secrecy.

    b) Many years/banks/denied/deposits/criminal sources.

    c) Over 40 years/Swiss banks/successful/resisting/change/rules.

    d) Doubtless the General Manager/Crédit Suisse/wishes/more careful/selecting/manager/Chiasso branch.

    e) Banks/warned/end relations/clients/identities/unclear.

    f) Many people feared/loss/secrecy/result/money/withdrawn/the banks.

    g) Crédit Suisse managed/cover its losses/hidden reserves.

    h) Chiasso scandal/opportunity/National Bank/pressure/Swiss commercial banks/tighten up their rules.

2. Supply any suitable word for each blank space.
   The numerous scandals in Swiss banking, of ...... the Chiasso affair is the largest and most widely ......, have been attributed by some financial experts ...... inadequate training and the ...... of the banks to adapt to rapid changes that ...... hit the world economy since 1970.

   Since ...... time, money has poured ...... Switzerland from numerous .... Petrodollars, Eurodollars, Italian lire, sterling and US dollars have all flowed in, some of the currencies ...... literally carried across the Swiss border in suitcases. The owners of this money were looking for quick profits, and as a result, bankers were tempted ...... entering unfamiliar ...... such as foreign exchange speculation and other risky real estate ventures. Many of the bankers got their fingers burned, and some even ...... suicide when their projects failed and their banks folded ......

3. Complete these sentences with suitable words.

   a) The new pact between the Central bank and the commercial banks provides ...... a substantial tightening ...... of the regulations.

   b) The Swiss have been regularly requested ...... foreign governments to give police access ...... information about certain accounts.

   c) ...... my view, Switzerland was irresistible ...... certain wealthy foreigners because of its system of numbered accounts.

   d) Italians working in Switzerland exchanged their Swiss francs ...... lire ...... a rate higher than the official one in Milan.

   e) The banks have promised not to employ agents abroad ...... a view ...... organizing capital flights.

   f) At the border, special police units sometimes take cars apart in their search ...... smuggled currency.

   g) The Italians are likely ...... react well ...... the new developments if the smuggling of currency ...... the Italian border ...... southern Switzerland is brought ...... a halt.

D Oral Work

1. Argue for or against the following debating theme:
   'The Swiss commercial banks have justifiably acquired a world-wide reputation for efficiency and discretion. Everyone concerned should have left the banks alone and let them put their own house in order.'

2. Discussion Topics

   a) What are the main services a bank should provide?

   b) Is it desirable that the banks in a country should be state-owned? Give reasons for your answer.

   c) Discuss the strengths and weaknesses of the banking system in your own country.

   d) Which foreign banking system do you most admire? Give reasons for your answer.

E Writing Exercises

1. 'Secrecy is one of the "pillars" of any banking system.' Discuss.

2. Analyze critically the operation and services of your own bank.

3. Some people consider that a banker's life is extremely dull and not terribly challenging intellectually. To what extent do you agree with this judgement?

4. Summarize the main facts of the 'Chiasso scandal'. The relevant passage begins on line 75, and ends on line 103. You should write your summary in about 60–80 words.

The World Bank

Preparation

1. What is the main function of the World Bank?
2. Some countries in the world are often described as being 'poor', while others are termed 'developing'. Do you think this is a useful distinction to make? If so, what are the distinguishing features of each category of country?
3. World Bank officials often talk of 'middle-income' countries. Give the names of countries which might be included in this group.
4. What does the term 'fertility rate' mean when applied to a country as a whole? In which countries is the rate of fertility high and in which low?

The World Bank is one of the major channels through which development aid is passed from the industrial West to the poor and developing nations of the world. Its scale of operations is vast, which is why its lending programme exceeds $7 billion a year, and its
5 workforce numbers about 4,500.

In the last decade, important changes have taken place in the size of the Bank's operations and in the emphasis of its lending policies. Few people would deny, furthermore, that the President of the Bank, Mr Robert McNamara, has played an important role in bringing
10 about the changes.

What immediately strikes anyone looking at the lending figures over the last ten years is the tremendous expansion in the Bank's loan programme. This has increased from $1 billion to nearly $7 billion. The figure includes 'hard loans' which are made at current rates of
15 interest, and 'soft loans' which are allocated to poor countries at concessionary rates, and usually channelled through the Bank's affiliate, the International Development Association (IDA).

In deciding the emphasis of its lending policy, the Bank has had to take into account the 'population explosion' which is occurring in
20 many poor countries of the world. It is a fact that the fertility rate of poor countries is often very high. This is one of the main reasons for these countries remaining poor. Unfortunately, wide-ranging contraception programmes do not usually reduce this rate because there is a strong and deeply-rooted tradition among people in these
25 countries to have big families. The large family unit, it is believed, brings greater financial stability.

What the Bank discovered — this was a revolutionary idea — was that there was a link between economic and social development, on the one hand, and a reduction in fertility rate, on the other. Thus, by
30 improving basic health services, by introducing better nutrition, by increasing literacy, and by promoting more even income distribution in a poor country, a lower and more acceptable fertility rate would be achieved.

This 'advance in thinking', to use Robert McNamara's words,
35 persuaded the Bank to change its overall lending strategy. Where

previously it had concentrated on the big infrastructure projects such as dams, roads and bridges, it began to switch to projects which directly improved the basic services of a country. There was a shift, if you like, from building dams to digging water holes to provide clean
40 water.

A second reason for the change in approach was that the Bank had learned a bitter lesson from projects financed in the 1960s. Many of its major capital investments had scarcely touched the lives of the urban and rural poor, nor had they created much employment. The projects
45 did not have the 'trickle down' effect they have in industrialized countries. Instead, the huge dams, steel mills and so on were left as monuments to themselves.

This redirection of its lending has meant that the Bank has tended to support labour-intensive activities rather than capital-intensive
50 ones, both in rural and urban areas. There is a better chance, in the first case, that its funds will benefit the bottom 40% of a country's population. The bank is also looking at ways of stimulating the growth of small businesses in many developing countries, since this would create employment opportunities for people with low incomes.
55 The major thrust of the Bank's efforts is directed towards improving conditions in poor countries. The Bank sees it as a moral

The World Bank and its affiliate, the International Development Association, are helping to finance a complex system of canals, etc. to distribute irrigation waters in West Pakistan. The overall scheme is known as the Indus Basin Scheme and is the largest irrigation system in the world. This is Ghanda Khan, an operator of tubewells in the Mangla area.

This picture on the cover of the 1977 World Bank annual report shows labourers harvesting sorghum in Upper Volta. This illustrates the shift of attention by the Bank to rural development and labour-intensive activities.

duty of developed countries to help those living in conditions of absolute poverty. Mr McNamara has publicly stated that he trusts 'civilized peope will never allow themselves to reach a stage where
60 they will watch on their colour TV sets other less fortunate nations perish.'

While retaining the priority of helping poor countries clearly in mind, the Bank also assists middle-income countries. What these need, above all, is a constant flow of investment capital, and they are
65 quite prepared to pay market rates for it. This 'investment flow' the Bank will provide. On such investments, the Bank earns an average return of 8% annually. It must be remembered that, although many of its loans are on concessionary terms, the Bank is also a hard-headed agency, not a welfare institution. It tries to increase the productivity
70 of these middle-income countries so that the loans 'earn the amount required to service them'.

Being such a big and obvious target, the Bank has often come under fire. For example, its officials have been taken to task for using the Concorde supersonic aircraft so frequently; about 500 times in
75 one year. Also, the large growth in the organization's personnel has not pleased some US critics.

A more substantial criticism has concerned the President's policy of setting annual targets for lending to specified countries. This could lead to a deterioration in the quality of loans, some say. One former
80 Bank official has said: 'rather than encourage growth for its own sake, the Bank should begin to think of itself less as a foreign aid agency and more of a financial "deal maker" combining official with private resources for specific purposes.'

Finally, some people maintain that the impact of the projects
85 funded by the Bank has been modest. When one looks around the world at countries that have successfully transformed to industrial status, for example Hong Kong, or have greatly improved the well-being of their peoples, for example China, it seems that one should beware of overestimating the Bank's impact. In the case of
90 Hong Kong, change has come about as a result of a trade offensive, the purpose of which has been to flood Western markets with cheap goods made by capitalist methods of production; in the case of China, change has come from radical social reorganization following an armed revolution.

Language Notes

Line 8	*The President of the Bank*: up to the present, all the Bank's presidents have come from the US, which has prompted some people to call the World Bank presidency a US appointment!
Line 28	*There was a link between ......*: an alternative for *link* would be *correlation*.
Line 55	*Thrust*: focus.
Line 58	*Absolute poverty*:defined by the World Bank as: 'A condition of life so characterized by malnutrition, illiteracy, disease, squalid surroundings, high infant mortality and low life expectancy as to be beneath any reasonable definition of human decency.'

A Comprehension

1. In what sense is the World Bank a 'channel'?
2. How extensive are the Bank's operations?
3. What is a 'soft loan'? Why do you suppose the World Bank makes this type of loan?
4. Why are birth control programmes not very effective in controlling population growth in poor countries?
5. How has the Bank modified its lending policy recently? Why has this change in emphasis taken place?
6. 'The huge dams, steel mills and so on were left as monuments to themselves' (l.46). What does the writer mean by this statement?
7. In what way does the need for capital of a middle-income country differ from that of a poor country?
8. What point is the writer trying to make when he quotes the examples of Hong Kong and China?

B Vocabulary

1. Circle the number next to the most suitable interpretation of the word in *italics*.

   a) The Bank decided to change its overall lending *strategy*.
      (i) terms   (ii) policy   (iii) amount

   b) There was a *shift from* building dams to digging water holes.
      (i) change in emphasis from   (iii) lack of interest in
      (ii) strong preference for

   c) The projects did not have the *trickle down* effect they have in industrialized countries. This means:
      (i) that relatively few people in the borrowing countries benefited from the projects.
      (ii) that the industrialized countries used the money far more wisely.
      (iii) that the projects were not really worthwhile in themselves.

   d) The Bank is looking for ways of *stimulating* the growth of small businesses.
      (i) enlarging   (ii) financing   (iii) encouraging

   e) The World Bank is a *hard-headed* agency.
      (i) stubborn   (ii) tough   (iii) realistic

   f) Being such a big and obvious *target*, the Bank has often come under fire.
      (i) organization with power   (iii) focus of attention
      (ii) object to attack

   g) Bank officials have been *taken to task* for using Concorde so frequently.
      (i) interrogated   (ii) dismissed   (iii) criticized

h) The *impact* of the projects *funded* by the Bank has been modest.
   - (i) effect
   - (ii) amount
   - (iii) total
   - (i) proposed
   - (ii) financed
   - (iii) set up

i) In the case of Hong Kong, change has resulted from *a trade offensive*.
   - (i) unfair competition in foreign markets
   - (ii) a policy of constant price-cutting
   - (iii) a sustained effort to win overseas markets

2. Here are some short extracts from a World Bank booklet. Explain briefly what each italicized word or phrase means.

   a) The Bank's charter *spells out* certain basic rules that govern its operations. It must lend only for productive purposes, and *pay due regard to* the prospects of repayment ...... Except in 'special circumstances', loans must be for *specific* projects. ...... And the Bank's decisions to lend must be based *only on economic considerations*.

   b) Assume, for example, that technical staffs of the government and the Bank agree that improvements in the road system are *a priority need* for attainment of the country's development goals. After some preparatory work, the Bank will send a staff *mission* to make a *thorough appraisal* of all aspects of the project.
   The approval of a loan does not end the Bank's involvement. In most cases, the borrower seeks *bids*, on the basis of international competition for the goods and services required. The Bank releases money only as needed to meet *verified expenditures* on the project.

   c) Member governments own and control the Bank. Every member *subscribes to* shares in an amount roughly based on its relative economic strength. The World Bank and the IDA are controlled by a Board of Governors, and 20 full-time Executive Directors. Most functions of the Governors are *delegated to* the Executive Directors. In practice, most decisions are taken on the basis of a *clear consensus* rather than by formal vote.

   d) The Bank provides a large amount of technical assistance to countries by administering *feasibility studies*, many of which lead to projects financed by the Bank and IDA.

3. Complete the sentences using an appropriate form of the words in *italics*.

   a) *vast*   The ...... of the Bank's resources does not mean that it throws money away.

   b) *deny*   The ...... of aid to poor countries is an unwise policy.

   c) *expansion*   The Bank has greatly ...... its lending in recent years.

   d) *concessionary*   As a ...... to some countries, interest rates on loans are below market rate.

e) *affiliate* About 130 countries are ...... to the Bank.

f) *explosion* In many countries, the population is ...... at an ever-increasing rate.

g) *fertility* Many rural programmes are aimed at making the land more ....

h) *economic* The Bank expects countries to use its funds ......, but this is not always the case.

i) *nutrition* The ...... value of certain foods is well-known.

j) *literacy* In some countries, as much as 60% of the population is not ....

k) *literacy* People who cannot read or write are said to be ....

l) *bitter* Poverty and harsh living conditions often ...... people.

m) *benefit* South Korea and Taiwan are both ...... of World Bank aid.

n) *institution* The Bank has tried to ...... better monitoring of its projects.

o) *deteriorate* In real terms, the condition of the poor in most countries has ....

p) *resources* In rural areas, technical experts often need to be extremely ...... and creative.

C Language Practice

1. Here is a short dialogue between a Bank official and a journalist who is interviewing him. Write a report of the conversation, using some of the verbs listed in the box.

| admit |
| apologize |
| remind |
| reassure |
| answer |
| insist |
| point out |
| confide |
| say |
| enquire |
| maintain |
| agree |
| ask |
| suggest |
| deny |

Journalist: Isn't it true that many of your projects have not been completed in time and have exceeded their budgets?

Bank official: To some extent, that's true. Because of inadequate planning, and in some cases, bad judgement, there have been some heavy cost overruns. But don't forget, we are oganizing and administering a vast number of projects throughout the world.

Journalist: I still say the Bank has a poor record in this respect. Take your public utility projects. The average completion time overrun has been about 50%.

Bank official: Absolute nonsense! It's more like 30%. I'd advise you to approach us, in future, if you want to get accurate statistics.

Journalist: I still think the Bank should keep a closer check on its projects.

Bank official:	We are doing everything in our power to see that money is not wasted. And I can tell you, between ourselves, that steps are being taken to monitor our projects even more carefully in future.
Journalist:	Do you mind if I put a final question?
Bank official:	I'm sorry. I hope you don't think I'm rude, but I must rush off to a committee meeting this minute.
Journalist:	I quite understand. Perhaps we can meet again this time next week.

2. Write out these sentences, using the most suitable tense or form of the verbs in brackets.

a) Last year, the wheat needs of people in Africa's Sahelian region could (meet) by a twentieth of the wheat Europeans (use) to feed their cattle.

b) By 1982, it (expect) that the World Bank (lend) almost $12 billion to member countries.

c) It is no use (provide) money for projects unless these are carefully planned.

d) Robert McNamara has been successful in (shift) the focus of aid away from transport, power and communications projects. Despite (criticize) by some experts, he has continued (urge) Bank officials (concentrate) more on agricultural development and urban renewal.

e) Senior Bank officials resent (attack) for (use) the Concorde airline too frequently.

f) It is essential that the productivity of the urban poor (increase).

g) The industrialized nations should be discouraged from (set up) trade barriers against the exports of developing countries.

h) The first step involves (prepare) a comprehensive study of the economy. The report which (draw up) is used by the Bank (provide) a basis for its decisions.

i) By (put) a photograph (show) the harvesting of sorghum in Upper Volta on the cover of its annual report, the Bank intended (draw) attention to its rural development activities.

j) At present, developing nations (urge) by the Bank (invest) more resources in labour-intensive projects.

k) It (think) by most experts that agriculture is the key to (improve) the living standards of the poor in many countries.

l) It is time people (realize) the seriousness of the population problem.

3. Complete the passage by supplying any suitable word for each blank space.

The difficulty ...... getting funds through the US congress is hardly likely to disappear during the next ...... years, and will inevitably put the Bank's capital requirements ...... considerable pressure. The next issue ...... the Bank's shareholders will be a general capital increase. Without this, it will not even be able to ...... its present lending programme in real terms.
...... or not the Bank gets enough money to be able to increase its lending will ...... be a key feature shaping it in the next five years. There is, ..., another ...... which I would argue is even more important. The Bank has increased enormously its ...... of operations. Its lending programme is now approaching seven ...... dollars. It has also started to direct its efforts ...... specific problems of economic development where the solutions have as ...... to do with the social and political structure of less developed nations ...... with their inadequate infrastructures. The big question is ...... the Bank can turn itself from being a body that lent money to build dams ...... a body which can help less developed nations to help ....

D Oral Work

1. Argue for or against the following debating themes:

   a) 'The efforts of the World Bank to combat poverty, though praiseworthy, are doomed to fail because world population growth will not be contained.'

   b) 'The spectre that stalks the world is not poverty; it is the greed of the developed, industrialized nations.'

2. Discussion Topics

   a) Eight hundred million people live in what the World Bank calls 'absolute poverty'. How would you personally define this state?

   b) 'A major transfer of wealth to developing nations occurred when OPEC countries dramatically raised the price of oil. Less developed countries, with no oil, can only try to obtain a 'larger slice of the cake' by using moral arguments.'
   Analyze and comment on this point of view.

   c) 'In order to help the exports of developing countries, the richer, industrialized nations should be prepared to allow certain of their own industries to contract, and even disappear, as a result of competition from these countries. It is an irrational approach of industrial nations to say "Let's block off these imports" because, after all, they need the Third World as much as it needs them.'

   'In many countries of the world, it is not international aid in the form of cheap loans that is needed, but political, economical and social change.'
   Discuss these points of view.

E Writing Exercises

1. Study this table showing Bank and IDA lending over a ten-year period. Using information gained from the text, and any other knowledge you may have, write comments and interpretations of these statistics.

   For example, you could say:

   In the 1967–71 period, virtually no Bank funds were spent on specific population projects. In 1977 alone, 1% of Bank lending was devoted to such schemes, These figures probably show an increasing awareness by the Bank of the need to control population growth.

Bank and IDA lending by principal sectors, 1967–77

(US$ millions. Fiscal years.)

| | 1967–71 | | 1972–76 | | 1977 | |
	Average	%	Average	%	Amount	%
Agriculture	$ 294	17	$1,163	25	$2,308	33
Development finance companies	179	11	434	9	756	11
Education	69	4	230	5	289	4
Industry	50	3	451	10	737	10
Nonproject	109	6	320	7	217	3
Population	2	—	28	1	47	1
Power	403	24	613	13	952	14
Technical assistance	2	—	12	—	17	—
Telecommunications	86	5	141	3	140	2
Tourism	6	—	32	1	99	1
Transportation	457	27	955	21	1,048	15
Urbanization	1	—	66	1	158	2
Water supply & sewerage	54	3	197	4	301	4
Total	$1,712	100	$4,643	100	$7,067	100

Note: Details may not add to totals due to rounding.

2. Discuss what contributions an individual can make towards helping those people living in conditions of 'absolute poverty'.

3. Summarize the section of the text dealing with the changing emphasis of the Bank's lending policy. This begins on l.6 and ends on l.54. Write your summary in 100–120 words.

East-West Trade — the problem of COMECON's debts

Preparation

1. Why is the USSR heavily in debt to US and Western creditors?
2. What kinds of goods does the USSR need to import from the West?
3. From the point of view of Western countries, what can be gained
   — and lost — by trading with the USSR and its satellites?

East–West trade is going through difficult times these days, and the
going could get even tougher in the years ahead. Comecon[1] had a
very large trade deficit with the West in 1978, and most countries in
this group are deeply in debt. They owe, it is estimated, about $50
5 billion, of which $20 billion represents money borrowed from
Western banks. By the early 1980s, Comecon's total indebtedness
could be anything from $60 billion to $80 billion.

Most Comecon countries need Western equipment, technology and
food. Russia, for instance, wants to develop areas in the east *exploit*
10 (especially Siberia) and also the far north where there are rich sources
of energy and raw materials. The cost of such projects is immense. *huge*
Naturally, the satellite countries will contribute some of the necessary
finance and technology, but the West has also been called in to help.
Besides making large purchases abroad for equipment to be used in
15 these capital projects, Russia buys from the West large quantities of *x substantial*
products like agricultural chemicals and food. Because of bad *x considerable*
yields harvests, it has also had to make massive purchases of grain from the
US from time to time.

The staggering increase in Comecon debt has made Western
20 creditors rather nervous; their uneasiness has been catching since
some of the countries themselves have begun to curb their imports
from the West. In 1977, the USSR, obviously worried that it was
plunging too far into debt to the capitalist countries, began a cutback
in spending. They cut out of their five-year plan, for example, an
25 expensive pulp and paper facility which was to have been designed
by a US company and they also put off a number of other US–Soviet
projects.
    In the West, there is an *anxious* uneasy feeling among bankers that lending
to Comecon has been too great, too fast, and even that the interest
30 rates charged have been too low. The bankers do not expect countries
to default on their debts; they do believe, however, that debt service
could be a serious problem for some countries. It is said that as much
as 40% of Poland's hard currency earnings will go towards servicing
its debt and paying interest.
35   The problem of Comecon debt has been to some extent created by
the US and Western European countries. These have eagerly sought *energetically*
deals with Comecon. However, because of various difficulties US
companies experience in trading with the USSR (mentioned below),
it is the European firms who have been more aggressive in their
40 efforts to get Soviet business. Some Americans claim, moreover, that
allege

1. The Comecon countries are: Russia,
Bulgaria, Czechoslovakia, East
Germany, Hungary, Poland,
Romania.

69

the Europeans have not only tried to underbid US competitors, but have even been prepared to sign contracts at breakeven prices.

Undeniably, the Soviet Union needs government-backed American credits for its energy projects and to exploit its raw material
45 resources. One snag, nevertheless, for US corporations is that the 1974 US Trade Act makes it impossible for the Export-Import bank to finance Soviet purchases of industrial equipment such as drills, pumps, steel pipes, etc. with low interest guaranteed credits. All US–Soviet trade must be financed at commercial bank interest rates.

50 Another restriction on this trade has been the US government's reluctance, at certain times, to grant companies export licences to sell high-technology equipment to the Russians. For example, the Control Data Corporation planned to sell a $13 million computer to the USSR — it would be used for weather forecasting, said the Russians — but
55 the US government stepped in smartly to cancel the deal. Considerations of national security, while understandable, have often proved a stumbling block to clinching deals with the Soviet Union.

Some specialists in international trade believe that Comecon indebtedness could be diminished if Western countries pressed
60 ahead with joint industrial projects with Comecon countries so that eventually these could improve their export performance.

There have been some successful deals of this kind in the past. The Volga Automobile Plant in the Soviet Union was built with extensive Fiat participation and a great deal of imported equipment. Before
65 long, the plant had recouped its expenditure with its car exports to Comecon and the West.

The gas-for-pipes deal is another project involving the Soviets. Western companies from West Germany, Austria, Italy, France and the US supplied the Russians with about $3½ million worth of pipes
70 and other equipment for processing, storing and transporting gas. In exchange, the Soviets agreed to supply natural gas to six Western European countries until 1990, and even, in some cases, to the year

A Polish ship under construction in Scotland.

2000. The deal should bring the USSR about $30 billion worth of hard currency.

75 Other Comecon countries do not have grand projects on the Soviet scale. They look for smaller ones which will attract Western capital and technology, and thus enable them to modernize their industrial and agricultural production.

Yugoslavia has been the pacesetter in the field of industrial
80 co-operation with the West. It was one of the first Communist countries to seek Western licences. It was also very quick to appreciate the advantages of joint ventures (joint ownership of equipment, marketing and management). With these projects, as opposed to licence deals and co-production agreements, it is much
85 more likely that the Western partner will pass on improvements in technology and the marketing of products in the West.

Although East–West industrial co-operation is flourishing, the future for trade between the two is not bright. While the West frets about the mounting debts of Comecon, these Eastern bloc countries
90 find they are facing increased competition in Western markets from the more advanced countries of the developing world. More important still, some people feel that a great threat to East–West trade looms on the horizon. This is the possibility of a Soviet oil shortage.

According to some US experts, the Soviet Union could change from
95 an oil-exporting to an oil-importing nation some time before 1985. If

this proves true, East–West trade will be seriously affected, since about half the Soviet Union's hard currency earnings now come from oil. Also, the satellite countries, which now import most of their oil from the USSR, would be forced to spend their precious hard
100 currency on Middle East oil.

When we take all these factors into account, it seems clear that a big expansion in East–West trade cannot be expected in the next decade.

Language Notes

Line 2   *The going could get even tougher*: there could be even greater problems in the future.

Line 31   *Default on their debts*: fail to pay their debts.

A Comprehension

- 1. What projects in particular are causing Russia to go into debt with the West?
- 2. How have Comecon countries reacted in the face of their ever-increasing trade deficits with Western countries?
  3. What advantage do European countries have over the US in doing business with Comecon?
  4. Why did the US government block the sale of an expensive computer to the USSR (l. 50–57)?
  5. In what way did the Volga Automobile Plant provide hard currency for the USSR (l. 58–66)?
  6. What attracts the Yugoslavs to joint-venture projects?
  7. What two reasons are given for the poor prospects facing East–West trade?

B Vocabulary

1. Find words similar in meaning to those in *italics*, or briefly explain their meaning.

   a) The *staggering* increase in Comecon debt has made creditors nervous.

   b) Their uneasiness has been *catching*.

   c) Some Comecon countries have begun to *curb* their imports.

   d) The USSR was *plunging* too far into debt.

   e) It began a *cutback* in spending.

   f) They *put off* a number of joint projects.

   g) European countries have *eagerly* sought deals.

   h) Some European companies were accused of signing contracts at *breakeven* prices.

   i) The Soviet Union needs credits to *exploit* its raw material resources.

j) One *snag* for US companies has been the 1974 Trade Act.

k) Considerations of national security have proved a *stumbling block* to *clinching* deals.

l) The Volga Auto Plant *recouped* its expenditure from car exports to the West.

m) Yugoslavia has been the *pacesetter* in the field of industrial co-operation.

n) A great threat to East–West trade *looms* on the horizon.

2. The comments below have all been made in connection with the problem of Comecon debt. Try to explain what each italicized expression means.

a) The communist countries are likely to go *deeper into the red*.

b) Because of mounting debts, some Comecon countries have been *tightening their belts*.

c) Because of difficulties with the US, Russia decided to *tap* alternative sources of supply in Western Europe.

d) Joint-venture projects have *mushroomed* in Yugoslavia since 1967.

e) Yugoslavia started the trend of joint ventures. Other countries were *slower off the mark* but are now *following suit*.

f) The OECD countries had a *gentleman's agreement* concerning interest rates on loans to Comecon countries.

g) When the USSR started cutting back its imports, West Germany was the first to *feel the draught*.

h) The Europeans have carried out a vigorous *export drive* for Soviet business, and the competition has been *cut-throat*.

i) Although there are untapped reserves of oil in Siberia, the Russians might not be able to bring these new oil supplies *on stream* in time to avoid *the crunch*.

C Language Practice

1. Write other sentences similar in meaning to the ones below, using the sentence openings provided. Make any other necessary changes.

a) Very soon after Yugoslavia set up joint ventures, other countries followed suit.
No sooner ......

b) Whatever happens, the Comecon countries must not be allowed to go on piling up debts.
Under no circumstances ......

c) The Comecon countries must improve the quality of their goods if they wish to earn more hard currency.
Only by ......

d) Some people do not realize at all the size of Eastern Europe's trade deficit with the West.
   Little ......

e) It is a long time since experts have been so pessimistic about the future of East–West trade.
   Rarely ......

f) The one time when the Russians borrowed relatively little from the West was in 1974.
   Only in 1974 ......

2. Each blank space in the paragraphs below should be filled with either *a*, *an* or *the*, or left without any article at all. Decide which is appropriate.

a) [1]...... serious problem for [2]...... USSR concerns [3]...... enormous cost of getting [4]...... oil and other materials out of the ground. Much of [5]...... mineral wealth of Russia is to be found in [6]...... remote areas such as [7]...... far north and Siberia. [8]...... huge investment in infrastructure is required before [9]...... work can be done on [10]...... actual drilling and manufacturing.

b) [1]...... manufacturers of [2]...... electric motors throughout [3]...... European Community have agreed on [4]...... joint approach to [5]...... Commission for [6]......urgent action to halt the flood of [7]...... low priced products arriving from [8]...... Eastern bloc countries.

c) Problems centre on [1]...... supply of [2]...... cheap but good-quality standard motors in [3]...... 100 to 200 horsepower range which are easily substituted for British and [4]...... other European products in a variety of equipment from [5]...... machine tools to [6]...... ventilating machinery.

3. Complete these sentences with prepositions or other suitable words.

a) The Comecon countries will have to compete ...... developing countries ...... Western business.

b) Russia has entered ...... an agreement ...... the Davy Power Gas Company of Britain ...... the delivery of two methanol plants.

c) The USSR has purchased $166 million worth ...... equipment ...... the aid of Japanese credits. Japan ...... return received shipments of timber.

d) Eastern Europe's trade deficit with the West amounts ...... billions of dollars. Most of the countries are heavily ...... debt ...... Western banks.

e) The trading problems of Comecon countries result ...... the poor quality of their goods. These are often inferior ...... the competition.

f) The far north is rich ...... mineral resources, and the Russians are investing in plant and equipment to open ...... this territory.

g) ...... comparison ...... other Comecon countries, Russia finds it easy to raise funds ...... international money markets.

h) Western bankers think we should distinguish ...... countries which can service their debts easily and those which have gone too heavily ...... debt.

i) To solve its debt problems, Comecon could always opt ...... a squeeze and cut ...... on imports from the West.

j) Poland's bankers are having to resort ...... sophisticated tactics to raise finance ...... Western markets.

D Oral Work

1. Argue for or against the following debating themes:

   a) 'East Europe's inefficient economic system will keep it permanently one step behind the West. It will continue to import new technology and goods but it will not produce enough goods of a standard acceptable to the West.'

   b) 'If the West has money to lend, this should be to the developing world, not to Eastern Europe.'

2. Discussion Topics

   a) The Eastern bloc countries have been exporting to Europe cheap but good-quality standard motors in the 100 to 200 horsepower range. These can be substituted for European products in a variety of equipment from machine tools to ventilating equipment. The Eastern European manufacturers have been so successful that they now have 50% of the total EEC market. How should the EEC Commission react to this situation?

   b) In 1974, the US passed legislation restricting the amount of credit that could be given to the USSR unless that country liberalized its emigration policy. What do you think of this action by the US?

E Writing Exercises

1. 'It is in the West's interests to continue to make credits available to Eastern Europe and to show an understanding attitude towards Comecon's mounting debt. By doing so, Comecon countries will be able to maintain their level of imports and their present standard of living.'
   Discuss.

2. 'East–West trade cannot flourish in the foreseeable future. The political differences are too great, the competition is too strong, and the Soviet economy is too weak.'
   Discuss.

Economic Democracy — the Dutch VAD proposal

Many cartoons appeared in the national press, mostly critical of VAD (see also page 78). This one shows Prime Minister Joop den Uyl as a VAD-clad sorcerer, with a 'rich man' and a 'poor man'.

Preparation

1. Should employees be entitled, by law, to share in their company's profits?
2. What are some of the ways that workers can be given a share in a company's growing profits?
3. In many countries, employees who happen to work in profitable industries earn much more than those doing comparable work in relatively unprofitable ones. Is this justifiable or desirable?

One topic of conversation almost guaranteed to raise the blood-pressure of a European industrialist is that of economic democracy. Although interpreted in many ways, this means, essentially, that employees should have a reasonable share in their
5 companies' capital growth; in simple language, they should share in the profits of an enterprise. In some countries, schemes to increase the workers' share in profits have also been designed to change the ownership structure of companies.

Proposals for some form of economic democracy have been
10 introduced in many European countries, for example, the Netherlands, Denmark, West Germany and Sweden. The draft bill drawn up by the socialist government in the Netherlands was of special interest because it created great controversy both in that country and abroad. Entitled rather grandly the *Excess Profit*
15 *Participation Bill*, it was known familiarly as the 'VAD'[1] proposal. Although not yet law, it provides a fascinating example of one brand of economic democracy.

The VAD Proposal

Origins
20 The draft bill came into being because the Dutch government believed that companies in the Netherlands often made profits beyond what could be regarded as reasonable. These 'excess profits', it argued, should be redistributed to the working population as a whole. Another justification for the bill was that differences in
25 profitability between industries should not lead to different pay levels. There should be 'equal pay for equal work', and any surplus profits should not go just to workers in industries generating profits but should be shared among *all* workers.

Main provisions of the bill
30 Companies earning more than 250,000 guilders before tax annually (about $100,000) would have to pay a percentage of their profits into a fund which would be administered by the unions for the benefit of all workers. Profits from non-Dutch sources would be exempted, so multinational companies would only pay the levy on profits earned in
35 the Netherlands.

1. Vermogensaanwasdeling.

Companies liable for VAD would be allowed a fair return on their own capital. This was to be based on the average interest rate of selected government bonds plus 2%. On its remaining profits, a company would pay the VAD rate. This was to start at 10% and rise
40 to a figure of 18% in 1979. If productivity rose faster than wages or vice versa, this rate might be raised three percentage points or lowered two points. The maximum rate payable in 1979, after making these adjustments, would be 20%.

It is clear from the above that 'excess profits', as defined by the
45 Government, were the profits a company made after deducting a return on its equity. A part of these would be siphoned off in the form of VAD contributions.

Companies would transfer profits to the fund in the form of shares, and the workers would receive, after a number of years, a certificate
50 of participation in the fund. This could then be sold for cash.

The money accumulated in the fund would be used to improve pensions for all employees, except self-employed persons and public servants — the latter already have excellent pension schemes.

An example of how VAD works
55 Take a Dutch company with a shareholder's equity (capital, reserves and retained earnings) of f100,000, a maximum VAD contribution rate of 20% in 1980, profit before tax of f1,000,000, and a corporate tax of 47%.

Income before tax	f1,000,000
Corporate tax at 47% of f1,000,000	470,000
Income after tax	530,000
Deduction for return on shareholder's equity, [2]10% of f100,000 = f10,000	
VAD: 20% of f520,000	104,000
	426,000

The example shows that corporate tax (f470,000) plus VAD (f104,000) = f574,000. Thus, the combined tax plus VAD rate is
70 57.4%.

Reactions to the VAD proposal
Foreign companies, not unnaturally, loathed the whole idea. A group of powerful multinationals, including Shell, Philips, Unilever and Akzo, wrote a strong letter of protest to the Dutch government. They
75 emphasized that labour costs in the country were high, as were the employer social security contributions they had to pay. They also maintained that the general business climate in recent years had not been conducive to the earning of high profits. Other companies, both domestic and foreign, complained of the Government's generally
80 unsympathetic attitude to business which was reflected in the high rate of corporation tax — at that time about 47%.

A group[3] of foreign Chambers of Commerce sent a report to the government committee handling the bill. They claimed that the

2. This rate, in practice, would be fixed by the government.
3. The group included: the Japanese Chamber of Commerce; the Netherlands — British Chamber of Commerce; the Belgian — Luxembourg, German and Swiss Chambers of Commerce.

proposed legislation would 'inhibit the flow of foreign investments to
85   Holland' and that it would also result in a certain amount of
'disinvestment' on the part of existing foreign subsidiaries.

Finally, many businessmen were worried that the VAD levy would
reduce the amount of capital they would be able to reinvest in their
enterprises, thereby limiting their ability to modernize their
90   machinery and plants.

Language Notes

Line 2   *That of economic democracy*: *that* is used for stylistic
                reasons. It avoids repetition of *one topic*.
Line 10   *The Netherlands*: note that the article is used with
                several countries, e.g. the USSR, the USA, the UK
                and the Philippines.
Line 36   *Liable for*: a company is liable *for* tax, i.e. subject to
                it. Some people are liable *to* do stupid things when
                drunk, i.e. apt to do stupid things.
Line 46   *Siphoned off*: usually used of liquids which are
                drawn out of a container, e.g. soda siphon.
Line 80   *Unsympathetic*: showing no understanding or
                compassion for someone else. Do not use the word
                sympathetic when you mean *likeable*, *pleasant* or
                charming.

Economics Minister Ruud Lubbers shouts
after his foreign investors: 'Why are you
all running away?'

A Comprehension

1. What reasons did the Dutch government have for making the VAD proposal?
2. Which companies would have to pay VAD?
3. What basis was going to be used by the Government to determine 'reasonable profits'?
4. Some people in the Netherlands believed the proposed law would 'redistribute capital'. What argument do you think they used to support this view?
5. In what ways would the VAD levy benefit (a) employees, (b) the unions?
6. What were some of the objections made to this draft law?
7. What is the meaning of the word 'disinvestment'. (l.00)

B Vocabulary

1. Complete each sentence using an appropriate form of the word in *italics*.

   a) *implement* This idea is good but ...... of such a scheme will be difficult.

   b) *topic* Both industrial democracy and economic democracy are ...... issues at present.

   c) *capital* We should now ...... on the rise in share prices by selling some of our stock.

   d) *familiar* It will take time for me to ...... myself with this complex legislation.

   e) *convince* The spokesman for the foreign companies put forward their objections with great ....

   f) *retain* The ...... of some part of earnings by a company is a common practice.

   g) *draft* The ...... of legislation is usually a time-consuming process.

   h) *emphasise* Some heads of firms stated ...... that they would close down their plants if the bill went through.

   i) *special* ...... in company law was a wise thing for her to do.

   j) *essence* What they are saying, in ......, is that they will not invest resources in that country.

   k) *justification* We are ...... pleased with our company's record in Holland.

   l) *levy* VAD will be ...... on all companies subject to Dutch corporation tax.

2. The statements below were all made in connection with the VAD proposal. Explain the meaning of each word or phrase in *italics*.

   a) The proposed law will *operate retrospectively to* January 1976.

b) The shares in the fund will *remain blocked* for a number of years.

c) Specifically, the multinationals criticized the Government for not giving enough *incentives* to foreign companies in order to encourage *capital investment*.

d) The VAD proposal will affect decisions whether to *plough back cash flows*.

e) The foreign Chambers of Commerce were afraid that unless there were regular private *placements* outside the fund, then the fund would eventually acquire *a majority interest in* the country's most profitable companies.

f) One suggestion was that VAD was an attempt to *soak* the rich companies.

3. Circle the number next to the most suitable answer.

a) The blood-pressure of a European industrialist will probably be raised because:
   (i) the idea of profit-sharing is very new to him.
   (ii) talk of economic democracy usually makes him feel rather ill.
   (iii) discussion of the topic tends to arouse strong feelings in him.

b) A draft bill is:
   (i) a preliminary outline of legislation.
   (ii) a very complicated law.
   (iii) a proposal on which there will be a vote.

c) The writer uses the word 'grandly' (l.14) because:
   (i) he is impressed by the dignified title of the bill.
   (ii) he is aware this is a government bill.
   (iii) he thinks the bill has a long, solemn title.

d) The general business climate had not been conducive to the earning of high profits (l.78). This sentence means:
   (i) companies had not made any profits for some length of time.
   (ii) companies had found it difficult to make profits because of unfavourable conditions.
   (iii) companies had realized their profits were steadily declining.

e) The proposed legislation would *inhibit* the flow of foreign investments to Holland.
   (i) cancel   (ii) restrict   (iii) eliminate

C Language Practice

1. Make sentences from these notes.

a) Concept/economic democracy/interpreted/different ways.

b) Widespread belief/employees/entitled/share/profits.

c) Aim/VAD proposal/siphon off/excess profits/companies/Netherlands.

d) Very small companies/exempted/VAD contributions.

e) Recommended/draft bill/retroactive/January 1976

f) Dutch government/criticized/foreign companies/no encouragement/capital investment.

g) Opinion/certain businessmen/Dutch government/unsympathetic/problems/foreign companies/Holland.

h) If/VAD proposal/become law/probable/foreign investment/Netherlands/decreased.

i) Estimated/24% to 30%/industrial exports/foreign companies/the Netherlands.

2. Write out these sentences using the most appropriate tense or form of the word in brackets. Make any other necessary changes.

a) There is no (deny) the fact that Holland (consider) by foreign companies until recently an attractive country for (set up) a subsidiary.

b) We would suggest (inform) the government that expansion of existing facilities will slow down particularly when companies have the option (expand) facilities in countries where a more favourable policy towards foreign investment (pursue).

c) A foreign investor who had considered (invest) in the Netherlands would have had to take into account the effects of VAD when (calculate) the return on his investment.

d) If the VAD proposal (put into effect), the fund (accumulate) a vast stock of shares in Dutch companies by 1980.

e) Essentially, the new law involved (siphon off) the excess profits of companies.

f) The foreign Chambers of Commerce have no intention (interfere) in the internal politics of Holland nor (they, wish) to seem (they, issue) threats to the government.

g) Although the unions have persisted (try) to get the rate of levy (increase), they have not managed (do) this.

h) Some people say the Dutch government failed (appreciate) the contribution of the multinationals towards (create) employment and exports.

i) Personally, I do not believe foreign companies should be made (share) their profits, but I am sure many of them would not object (their employees, share) in a scheme which directly benefited them.

j) When foreign companies first (hear) of the VAD proposal, it (must, cause) them a great deal of apprehension.

k) Many influential businessmen urged the government (lower) the rate of corporate tax, but it refused (comply) with their request. Other people did not regard the rate (be) excessively high. Indeed, they expect it (go) higher in the future.

D Oral Work

1. Argue for or against the following debating theme.

> 'VAD was a wise legislative proposal. It was admirable in conception and entirely appropriate for a country such as the Netherlands which is host to a great number of wholly-owned foreign subsidiaries.'

2. Discussion Topics

   a) At one point during the discussions of the VAD bill, the Dutch unions were asking that the levy should be set straightaway at 50%. To what extent do you think they were justified in their request?

   b) VAD was only one element in the Dutch government's wide-ranging incomes policies. The Government not only wanted earnings differentials between industries to be as small as possible, but also earnings differentials between the lowest and highest paid workers in *each* industry to be 'reasonable'. The tax system also was to be used as an instrument in levelling off incomes — the maximum rate at that time was 72% for incomes over £30,000 p.a. The Dutch government saw VAD as a first step: 'It is only a beginning because the excess profit participation scheme (VAD) only pertains to the increase of capital and not to capital now existing.'
   —What are your personal views on this particular industrial stategy?

   c) What arguments could heads of foreign enterprises use to persuade the Dutch government to alter its policy regarding company profits?

E Writing Exercises

1. You are the Financial Director of Universal Glass Ltd., an enterprise specializing in building materials. Your organization is a subsidiary of a multinational company whose head office is in Chicago, USA. You have just received information about the VAD proposal. Realizing its consequences for your firm, you decide to write immediately to the Executive Vice-President of your company, telling him about the draft bill and recommending a course of action which Universal Glass should follow.

2. In about 60–80 words, write a statement about the VAD proposal which could have been used by the Dutch government as a press release. The text you draft should inform the Dutch public that a profit-sharing scheme is under consideration and give a general idea of the nature of the proposal.

Construction Contracts in the Middle East

Preparation

1. Many Middle East countries are currently earning vast revenues from oil. How do you think the money should be spent? (Bear in mind that oil reserves are finite.)
2. From a foreign company's point of view, what are some of the problems and risks of doing business in Middle East countries?
3. What kinds of business opportunities does Saudi Arabia offer to foreign companies?

Oil has provided many Middle East countries with the means of financing ambitious development plans. As a result of these, multi-million dollar contracts are on offer to foreign civil engineering and construction companies. Some of the contracts relate to the
5   building of port and harbour complexes, dry docks, motor-ways and similar schemes which will set up the basic infrastructure of these countries. Others involve expensive capital projects such as power plants, refineries, petro-chemical installations and electrification networks. In Kuwait, one contract offered the challenge of creating an
10   entirely new town.

    Projects of this scale and complexity are potentially very lucrative for the companies chosen to implement them; they stimulate business activity in the region and also offer opportunities to small and medium-sized firms in the form of subcontracting work and
15   consultancy assignments.

    Nevertheless, while the rewards of doing business in the Middle East are considerable, so also are the risks. The foreign contractor is negotiating in a buyer's market. He finds out, sometimes too late and the hard way, that the terms of his contract are weighted in favour of
20   the Arab employer. There are, he learns, few easy pickings in these countries for foreign firms, but plenty of pitfalls for the unwary and inexperienced businessman.

    To illustrate just how tough it can be to do business in the Middle East, we shall take a look at the problems faced by contractors in
25   Saudi Arabia.

    In this country, as in most other Middle East regions, fixed price, lump-sum contracts are the rule. These create many headaches for the foreign contractor. It must be remembered that a company is often tendering for a project which will take three or four years to complete.
30   The contractor is in effect selling his product before he makes it — not afterwards. He cannot therefore adjust his price to changes in costs. When making a tender, he must make allowances in his quoted price for possible increased costs, but it is far from easy to calculate how great these will be.

35   One factor the contractor must take into consideration when making a bid is the rate of inflation in Saudi Arabia. Unfortunately, this is impossible to estimate accurately because reliable statistics are not available. If a tender is to appear reasonable, a contractor cannot

really allow for an annual increase of more than 25%, yet the current
40 rate of inflation may be exceeding that figure, and who can say what
it might be in three or four years time.

Another snag is that costs may rise because of changes in
specifications made by the ministry awarding the contract. Such
changes will often involve extra expense for the company concerned.
45 Disputes can arise leading to delays in the completion of the work. In
such cases, penalty clauses are sometimes invoked. Naturally, the
foreign contractor feels that he has been treated rather unfairly.

Foreign businessmen operating in Saudi Arabia believe that
escalation or revision clauses should be allowed in contracts. These
50 would take into account changes in wages, salaries, raw materials,
transportation costs, etc. However, the Saudis have, on the whole,
been against escalation clauses because they think these give the
contractor an open-ended licence to raise prices. From the foreign
company's point of view, a cost-plus contract is probably ideal
55 because it gives a guaranteed return for the work done.

The question of fair pricing of tenders came to a head in 1977 when
Saudi Arabia angrily rejected the 'inflated bids' made by Western and
Japanese groups for power projects in the country. Previous to this
decision there had been a growing feeling among Saudi officials that
60 their country was regarded as a soft touch by certain foreign
companies. The Saudis claimed that the companies were exaggerating
conditions in the Kingdom so as to inflate their tender prices. After
some rather public rows between the two sides, the Saudis began, as
a matter of policy, to award big contracts — including those for the
65 power stations — to Far Eastern construction companies, mainly from
India, Pakistan and South Korea. Explaining the rejection of the bids
for the power plants, a Saudi Minister of Planning said it proved his
country was not 'easy meat'.

The attitude of the companies was that the Saudis were suffering
70 from feelings of paranoia and exploitation while they ignored factors

Round the clock working, laying
concrete slabs at the Islamic port of
Jeddah, Saudi Arabia.

like the rate of inflation, high cost of living, bottlenecks in supplies
and bureaucratic slowness, all of which pushed up prices. Company
spokesmen also pointed out that tenders could be inflated because of
the commissions that needed to be paid to intermediaries. These
75 could vary from 5% to 35% of the contract value. Some of these critics
added that winning a big contract usually depended on a princely
personage getting a slice of the cake.

There were, to be sure, arguments on both sides. Certainly, there
have been at times huge gaps between estimates for a project drawn
80 up by independent consultants and the pricing of bids by companies
tendering for the contracts. The classic case is provided by the Philips
tender for a nationwide switching project in Saudi Arabia.
Sophisticated technology would have been used to increase the
number of telephones from 200,000 to 660,000. After one year's
85 negotiations, the final figure set by the Dutch company was 24 billion
riyals ($6.76 billion). This figure compared with that of 4 billion riyals
estimated by the Minister of Posts, Telegraphs and Telephones; a
staggering discrepancy in estimates!

Another difficulty for a foreign firm, especially if it is small or
90 medium-sized, is how to finance the bonds and related guarantees
connected with contract bids.

First, a company must meet the bid bond requirement. This takes
the form of a bank guarantee representing 1% to 2% of the total
contract value. The idea is to make sure the company has serious
95 intentions, and that it will not withdraw after it has been awarded
the contract. Most contractors do not object to the bid bond, although
it can be a substantial amount in the case of a big project.

The performance guarantees are a different matter. Generally set at
about 5% to 10% of the contract value, they are meant to ensure the
100 project is completed by the contractor. If the company drops out, the

Abha Airport, Saudi Arabia. The
departures hall.

money is surrendered. Because the bonds are unconditional, and thus payable upon demand, they have advantages from the Arab point of view. If a serious dispute with a contractor arose, the bond could be called in, thereby enabling the employer to avoid a long and costly
105   lawsuit.

These bonds can be a bugbear for all companies regardless of their size. When competing for a major project, the large company or group needs vast financial backing from banks or governments. Those who get full support have the edge over their competitors.
110   When more modest projects are offered, the small or medium-sized firm may find it gets frozen out of the market simply because it cannot get the capital quickly enough to finance these bonds. Banks may be unwilling to take the risk and because the bonds are unconditional, insurance companies tend to be cagey about lending
115   the money.

Even when companies are able to put up the bonds, they have the nagging worry that these are unconditional and therefore they have no real protection if they carry out their part of the bargain but the employer thinks otherwise for some reason. In recent years in Saudi
120   Arabia, very few of these bonds have been called in. Nevertheless, because of performance bonds, companies must raise substantial sums of money, then leave these tied up in projects for some length of time.

Language Notes

Line 36	*Making a bid*: an offer or a tender. A company bids or tenders *for* a contract.
Line 46	*Penalty clause*: this provides for some penalty, usually a sum of money, if the contractor fails to carry out a part of the contract.
Line 56	*Came to a head*: reached a critical point.
Line 70	*Paranoia*: persecution, victimization.
Line 111	*Frozen out of the market*: excluded because of the high cost of making a bid.
Line 114	*Cagey*: wary, cautious.

A Comprehension

1. Many civil engineering contractors see the Middle East construction projects as an 'exciting challenge'. What do you think they mean?
2. In most Middle East countries, a buyer's market exists. What effects does this have on companies doing business in these areas?
3. Explain briefly why Saudi officials favour fixed price rather than cost-plus contracts?
4. The Saudis turned down Western bids for power projects. How did they justify this action?
5. What did the example of the Philips company show?
6. Most foreign companies consider that performance bonds are in principle acceptable but in practice create real problems for companies operating in the Middle East. In about three to five lines, amplify this point of view.

B Vocabulary

tender
commissions
penalty clauses
escalation clauses
backing
estimates
projects
infrastructure
contractors
subcontracting
bottleneck
specifications
lucrative
fixed price

1. Choose words or phrases from the box on the left to complete the following sentences.

   a) Most ...... know that doing business in the Middle East is not easy. However, some of the big ...... offer an exciting challenge and can obviously be very ...... for a company.

   b) Ports, roads, airports, etc. are needed to establish the ...... of many Middle East countries. For such schemes, companies must have financial ...... from one or several banks.

   c) Delays in completing a project can occur. A ministry may decide on a change in ......, or there may be a ...... in supplies somewhere. Because of the delays, ... are sometimes invoked by the employer concerned.

   d) Most companies which ...... for contracts in the Middle East would like ...... to be included in the terms of contract. Because many contracts are offered on a ...... basis, companies generally make allowances in their ...... for additional expenses, for example, the rate of inflation and the high ...... which must be paid to intermediaries.

   e) Most large construction projects provide a great deal of ...... work for smaller firms.

2. Give synonyms for the italicized words in each sentence below, or briefly explain their meaning.

   Example: Projects of this $\left\{ \begin{array}{l} scale \\ \text{SIZE} \end{array} \right.$ can be lucrative.

   a) Big projects can be very *lucrative* for a contractor.

   b) In the Middle East, there are plenty of *pitfalls* for the inexperienced businessman.

   c) Usually, many companies *tender* for a project.

   d) Finding money for the guarantees is one possible *snag*.

   e) Few companies are given an *open-ended* licence to increase costs.

   f) The Saudis thought the Western bids were *inflated*.

   g) There was a *row* between the Government and the companies.

   h) *Sophisticated* technology is used by computer manufacturers.

   i) The *discrepancies* between official estimates and those of the companies can be very large.

   j) For small companies, the performance bond requirement can be a real *bugbear*.

   k) A company with superior products generally has the *edge* over competitors.

   l) The fact that the bonds are unconditional is a *nagging* worry for companies.

3. Interpreting words and phrases. Circle the number next to the most suitable answer.

a) When a foreign businessman 'finds out the hard way' (l. 19):
    (i) he usually loses money but gains experience.
    (ii) he gets what he wants by working very hard.
    (iii) he finds it difficult to break into the market.

b) A contract 'weighted in favour of the employer' (l. 19):
    (i) is written so that the foreign company gains no advantage from it.
    (ii) is a legal document which has been very badly drafted.
    (iii) has been drawn up so as to give the employer most of the advantages.

c) In these countries, there are 'few easy pickings' (l. 20):
    (i) almost no buyers for the goods offered.
    (ii) not many suitable business opportunities.
    (iii) not many possibilities for quick profits.

d) The Saudis felt their country was regarded as 'a soft touch' (l. 60):
    (i) weak in its treatment of foreigners.
    (ii) easy to exploit financially.
    (iii) friendly towards foreign companies.

e) 'Getting a slice of the cake' refers to (l. 77):
    (i) promises made by princes of the Kingdom.
    (ii) contracts awarded by officials of high status.
    (iii) payments made to people of high standing.

C Language Practice

1. Each blank space in the paragraphs below should be filled with either *a*, *an* or *the*, or left without any article at all. Decide which is appropriate.

a) [1]...... average Western woman is happy in [2]...... Kingdom of Saudi Arabia. [3]...... life is quite tolerable for her. [4]...... large proportion of expatriate wives have remunerative jobs or pursue [5]...... lucrative hobby. Demand for [6]...... labour is high, so that [7]...... women often find they have [8]...... more interesting work than at home. Husbands like their wives to go out to work when [9]...... wage packet is high. [10]...... alternative may be [11]...... lonely, bored wife cooped up in [12]...... home.

b) [1]...... chance to put aside something for [2]...... future is [3]...... incentive for many foreign workers. Also, for those who enjoy [4]...... desert and [5]...... sea, the country offers [6]...... excellent opportunities for weekends in the open air where [7]...... warmth and [8]...... sunshine are guaranteed. Indeed, [9]...... sunshine becomes excessive for much of [10]...... summer when temperatures rise above 40 degrees centigrade. But [11]...... Red Sea offers [12]...... magnificent coral reefs for [13]...... divers, and for those owning [14]...... robust vehicles, there is [15]......

possibility of [16]...... travel through marvellous desert scenery.
[17]...... security is excellent in this country. Like [18]......
householder, [19]...... traveller has nothing to fear.

2. Choosing appropriate language.

Below are some comments by foreigners working in the Middle
East. Rewrite each paragraph in a more formal style as if you were
writing to someone you did not know particularly well.

Example:

'You know, at times I think I must have been crazy to come out here. Sure, the money's great but life is a drag, and all you can see is sand, sand, sand.'	*'I sometimes think I was extremely unwise to come to this country. It is true that I earn a high salary but life here is extremely boring and all one seems to see is sand.'*

a) 'Over here, there's no way you can operate without a local
    partner. The catch is that all the good ones have been snapped
    up by foreign firms ages ago. Also you've got to watch out for
    agents. They're always saying they've got the ear of some
    Prince or they can fix things for you. Huh! that's a laugh!'

b) 'We're in a tricky situation at the moment. We'd like to go all
    out for this contract. It's for building pre-fabricated houses
    actually. But our bank's pussyfooting around. We've been
    waiting for over two months for the go-ahead from them'.

c) 'We work long hours, but we couldn't care a damn. There's not
    a thing to do in the evenings. No theatre. No concerts. Not a
    drop of alcohol is allowed. If you're caught drinking anything
    alcoholic, watch out! You know, we're only sticking it out here
    for the money. Phew! How I dread some of those summer
    months. The heat's murder!'

d) 'Don't worry. No one here will break into your apartment or
    mug you in the street. And your son won't be on drugs the
    moment he sets foot in school. Mind you, watch it when you
    drive. The roads are choked with cars and you can't go
    anywhere without seeing a nasty accident. As for the drivers
    . . . unbelievable! Worse than the Italians, and that's saying
    something. You know, my company won't give me a car. Not
    worth the risk, they say.'

D Oral Work

1. Argue for or against the following debating theme:
    'The Saudi Arabian approach to foreign contractors is tough but
    fair.'

2. Discussion Topic

    What special problems would you expect to encounter when doing
    business in Middle East markets that you might not find in other
    markets, e.g. the Far East, Europe or North America? Are there
    any particular advantages that the Middle East markets offer?

E Writing Exercise

Sending a cable back to Head Office.

In one of the smaller Middle East countries, a British construction company has recently made a tender for the building of a large apartment complex. The Managing Director of this company has been summoned unexpectedly to a meeting with the Deputy Minister of the Department concerned with the project. Read the dialogue below recording their discussion, then try to do the exercise which follows it.

Managing Director: If I understand you correctly, Minister, you were entirely satisfied with our plans and our company will be awarded the contract.

Deputy Minister: Now, wait a minute. Let me explain things clearly. We are entirely satisfied with your design for the building. Everyone praised it highly.

M.D.: So, what's the problem?

D.M.: In a word, price. Your bid was 10% higher than any of the others we received.

M.D.: Really, that surprises me. Where does that leave us?

D.M.: I'm afraid you'll have to cut your profit margin or look carefully at your estimates again. We're simply not willing to go over £12 million for the whole project.

M.D.: Well, that's disappointing.

D.M.: Look, we want your company to handle the project. You've got the experience in our country, the expertise . . . We like your work very much. We would make certain concessions . . .

M.D.: Oh yes?

D.M.: Yes, as a special concession, we could reduce the performance bond from 5% to 2%, and we could probably increase our progress payments as well. Would that help?

M.D.: It certainly would. Hmm, where do I go from here?

D.M.: Time's very short. Cable your planning department in Liverpool. Get them to go over the estimates again. See if they can cut costs by at least 10%. Anyway, if you can get your price down by at least that amount, then we're in business. But hurry up. I'd like an answer by next Monday — that's a week from now. I can't give you any longer than that . . .

Instructions: write the text of the Managing Director's cable to the Head of his Planning Department. Make sure the cable accurately reflects what was said in this discussion.

Product Liability Laws in the US and EEC Countries

Preparation

1. Should manufacturers be obliged by law to compensate their customers for any injuries their products cause, whether they have been negligent or not? In other words, should they be 'strictly liable' for their products?
2. Recently, in the United States, a psychiatrist was paralysed after striking his head on the bottom of a swimming pool. He was awarded damages of £1.25 million against the pool's manufacturers. Does the size of the award seem reasonable? And if so, why?
3. A pharmaceutical company produces a drug which is taken by pregnant women. Fifteen years later, a number of these develop a specific disease which has resulted from their taking the drug. Should the company be held responsible and pay compensation to all the victims?

What price should a manufacturer pay when one of his products causes injury because it is defective? This is always a difficult question to answer; in some circumstances, it is even difficult to decide whether a manufacturer is liable at all. Let us look at a few
5 cases heard in British and US courts. Here are four examples:

A In a 1975 British case, a man whose eye was destroyed by the rotary blade of his son's toy helicopter collected only the equivalent of about $10,000.

B In the US in 1977, a man from Michigan was awarded $154,000
10 after he had lost a finger while operating a lift truck.

C The manufacturer of a bench saw made for the US Navy in 1942, and originally equipped with the required safety guard, was ordered to pay $50,000 to a worker injured while using the machine in 1971. The award was made despite evidence that
15 the machine had been rebuilt by a dealer who had removed the safety guard.

D Recently a jury in Pittsburgh awarded more than $500,000 to a Pennsylvania coal miner who had been crippled while working. The company paying compensation was the National
20 Mine Service Corporation, the manufacturer of a coal shuttle car involved in the accident. Though other miners testified that the victim was not adequately trained and was operating the car improperly, the manufacturer was held liable.

When one compares case A with case B, it seems at first sight that
25 in the British case the victim was paid too little for his injury while in
the US case the victim was compensated very well indeed. In cases C
and D, the awards appear very high in view of the facts indicating
that the victim to some extent had contributed personally to his
injury.
30   In Western Europe the Common Market countries are now moving
towards product liability laws which will be harsher on business than
ever before. This is partly because of the tragic events during the
early 1960s when hundreds of infants in Britain and Germany were
born with deformities because their mothers, while pregnant, had
35 taken a drug called thalidomide.
    The EEC proposals are based on the legal concept of 'strict liability',
and, in this respect, they are modelled on the tough US product
liability laws. The term 'strict liability' means that if a product causes
injury because of a defect in manufacturing, a company is liable even
40 if it took all due care when making the product.
    A very controversial section of the proposals says that a
manufacturer is liable even for those defects that could not have been
foreseen 'in the light of the scientific and technological developments
at the time the item was put into circulation'. A ten-year limit is
45 proposed on a company's liability, probably to soften the severity of
this provision.
    As a result of the proposed strict liability concept, many people
believe that the EEC rules will create the same kind of 'product
liability' crisis in Europe that now exists in the US. There, awards in

In 1978 this picture of a model gondola
appeared in many British newspapers.
Many of the plastic models, imported
from Italy, were so badly wired that
they could give a fatal electric shock.
The public were warned of the danger
and the Department of Prices and
Consumer Protection served
summonses on firms who imported the
gondolas.

50 such cases are rising, and companies are having to pay soaring
premiums for product liability insurance, especially in high-risk areas
like pharmaceuticals, chemicals, automotive parts, and industrial
machinery generally. Smaller companies have found difficulty in
getting any insurance at all and a few such companies have had to
55 close down because of product liability claims.

Problems in the US have arisen from the judicial interpretation of
'defect'. In recent years, the courts have begun to hold manufacturers
liable for the full life of their product and for 'foreseeable' design
defects that might not appear until many years later (see example C
60 and the case of the bench saw). Many lawyers in the US oppose this
idea of the manufacturer's 'absolute liability'. They feel that some of
the manufacturer's liability should be transferred to the negligent
employer or employee, and that contributory negligence ought to be
allowed as a defence. US courts, for example, have held a perfume
65 manufacturer liable for burns sustained by somebody who poured
perfume on a lighted candle, to see how it would smell.

There is also pressure from many legal experts to allow
manufacturers a 'state of the art defence'. This means that they could
plead that a modern safety feature was not technologically available
70 when the product was originally manufactured. A member of the
American Bar Association has quoted the example of the Wright
brothers' airplanes built during the 1900s in order to illustrate his
view of the absurdity of the present state of the law: 'Suppose one of
those planes was still around and that it came down and injured
75 someone. The injured person under today's standards could argue
that the maker was at fault because the plane doesn't have the safety
features of a Boeing 747 jet'.

Strong support in the US has also come for a statute of limitations
beyond which a manufacturer would no longer be liable for injury
80 caused. Some favour ten years, as proposed in the EEC rules. They
point out that many lawsuits brought against industrial machine
manufacturers involve equipment more than twenty-five years old.

Leaving aside changes in the actual law itself, we can now turn to
the vexed question of the size of awards. Some limits on the size of
85 these is thought necessary in the US. Many of the big awards (over
$100,000) have substantially exceeded the courts' estimates of
'economic loss' — medical expenses, lost earnings, etc.

Large awards, now on the increase, are partly the result of the high
salaries in the US. They reflect its affluent society. They also stem
90 from the fact that comprehensive social security is still lacking in the
US so that a badly-injured person will have to pay for constant
medical attention for life, and this can cost a fortune.

A very important reason, however, for the size of awards in the US
is the country's system of contingency fees for lawyers. Under the
95 system, lawyers are paid nothing if they lose the case, but a third or
more of the award if they win. In other words, payment by results!
Of course, they have a big incentive not just to win but to squeeze
every last dollar from the court, in their own and their clients'
interests.

100 Many Europeans criticize the contingency fee system of paying
lawyers. They say that the system does not just compensate victims
for economic loss — and perhaps make some allowance for pain and
suffering — but it also provides a windfall profit for lawyer and

105   victim. American lawyers, on the whole, seem in favour of this system. They think it works in favour of the injured person. It leads to the law being interpreted on humanitarian grounds rather than strictly legalistic ones. A lawyer will risk spending a year or so trying to establish a legal precedent on behalf of a badly-injured person, especially if that person is likely to be awarded $1 million or more.

Language Notes

Line 20   *Coal shuttle car*: a car or carriage moving to and fro carrying coal.

Line 81   *Lawsuits brought against*: a person 'brings a lawsuit against' a company/takes a company to court/takes legal action against a company/sues a company.

Line 103   *Windfall profit*: unexpected financial gain.

A Comprehension

1. Why is the writer of this article critical of the award made by the jury in Pittsburgh (l. 26)?
2. The EEC proposals regarding product liability are not likely to be welcomed by European manufacturers. Why is this so?
3. In the United States, what effect have the tough product liability laws had on small companies?
4. What is 'contributory negligence'? Why would US manufacturers be glad to see this concept incorporated in their product liability laws?
5. What argument might someone in the US use to justify a 'statute of limitations'?
6. What are some of the factors accounting for the high awards granted by US courts to victims of defective products?
7. What is the contingency system of paying lawyers? Why do some US lawyers favour it?

B Vocabulary

1. Find suitable words for the blank spaces. Use the first-letter clues that have been provided.

    a) In the US, if a product causes an injury to someone because it is d......, a company is l...... in law, even if it took care when making the product.

    b) Large companies in the US have to pay very high insurance p...... to cover themselves against product liability claims.

    c) Many of the l...... brought by people against manufacturers have involved defects in very old machines.

    d) Some victims of defective products have received a...... in excess of $1 million.

    e) Under the proposed new law, a victim would not have to prove the company was n...... in some way, but simply that he was injured by the product.

    f) It is difficult for a judge to decide what amount of d...... is sufficient to c...... someone when he has suffered very great injury from a product.

    g) With the c...... f...... system of payment, a lawyer will often work harder on behalf of his c...... because the financial reward will be greater.

2. Interpretation of words and phrases. Circle the number next to the most suitable answer.

    a) Companies in the US are having to pay *soaring* premiums.
        (i) rising at a fast rate
        (ii) costing a great deal
        (iii) increasing at a steady pace

    b) It seems *at first sight* that in the British case the victim was paid too little.
        (i) after preliminary consideration of the matter
        (ii) after a quick evaluation of the law
        (iii) after first catching a sight of it

    c) The pharmaceutical and chemical industries are 'high-risk areas' because:
        (i) an enormous amount of risk capital is invested in these industries
        (ii) these industries are very competitive and therefore very risky.
        (iii) the possibility of their products injuring customers is higher than in many other industries.

    d) Manufacturers could *plead* a modern safety feature was not available at the time.
        (i) insist   (ii) argue   (iii) beg

    e) We turn to the *vexed* question of the size of awards.
        (i) irritating   (ii) controversial   (iii) critical

f) Many big awards have *substantially* exceeded the courts' estimates of economic loss.
   (i) easily   (ii) scarcely   (iii) considerably

g) In the context of the article, 'economic loss' means such things as:
   (i) loss of compensation by the courts
   (ii) loss of future earnings
   (iii) loss of earnings and medical expenses

h) Large awards reflect its *affluent* society.
   (i) wealthy   (ii) generous   (iii) humane

i) The size of awards *stems from* the fact that a comprehensive social security system is lacking in the US.
   (i) benefits from   (ii) produces from   (iii) results from

j) The lawyer will work hard to create a *legal precedent* for his client.
   (i) a special law relating to the individual
   (ii) a legal decision serving as a rule
   (iii) a law protecting individual rights

k) The contingency fee system provides *a windfall profit* for lawyer and victim. This statement implies that:
   (i) the lawyer and victim receive more money than they deserve
   (ii) the lawyer and the victim are entitled to the money they receive
   (iii) the lawyer and victim do not get as much money as they should

3. Complete the sentences using an appropriate form of the word in *italics*.

a) *product*   It is difficult to get skilled workers, so we try to increase the ...... of those we already have.

b) *injure*   Certain toys can be ...... to a child's health.

c) *liable*   The company denied ...... for the accident.

d) *cripple*   He received a ...... injury at work.

e) *victim*   Workers disobeying their union are sometimes ...... by their colleagues.

f) *foresee*   We shall not expand our factory capacity in the ...... future.

g) *critic*   Many lawyers are ...... of the EEC draft directive on product liability.

h) *inadequate*   The ...... of the present product liability law is recognized by everyone, hence the need for change.

i) *oppose*   Consumer associations and manufacturers are in ...... concerning this law.

j) *indicate*   The controversy surrounding the proposals is ...... of their importance.

k) *soar* Consumers are getting used to ...... prices.

l) *negligent* The fact that someone has ...... operated a machine has not often influenced US juries.

m) *expert* My lawyer has a great deal of ...... in product liability law.

n) *plead* The company has entered a ...... of guilty.

o) *fault* This product had a ...... wiring system.

p) *affluent* The ...... of certain sectors of the city strikes one's eye immediately.

q) *feature* We may expect a number of cases ...... pharmaceutical companies.

C Language Practice

1. Write out the sentences using the most appropriate tense or form of the word in brackets. Make any other necessary changes.

a) Unless the EEC (modify) its proposals, it will be unable (avoid) (create) the type of product liability crisis now (exist) in the US.

b) If legislation (base) on the present proposals, a large number of unreasonable claims would be bound (arise) from those (consider) themselves to be injured as a result of (use) defective products.

c) Most European manufacturers have resigned themselves to (accept) the strict liability principle, but they hope the courts will refrain (interpret) too generously the concept of 'defect'.

d) In some industries, companies will hesitate (introduce) new products for fear of (bring) upon themselves lawsuits.

e) One reason for the EEC (insist) (introduce) the strict liability concept is that it wishes to encourage firms (set up) better safety standards.

f) Letting manufacturers (evade) responsibility for (make) unsafe products is not a sensible policy.

g) A group of industrialists has requested that a 'state of the art' defence (allow). However, the members of this group are not optimistic of their proposals (accept).

h) The public should be made (realize) that (introduce) 'strict liability' laws may lead to prices (rise).

i) The government risks (do) lasting damage to successful companies if it (place) too heavy responsibilities on them.

j) There is a case to be made (fix) maximum amounts of an award.

k) Most consumer associations resent people (suggest) that the government (share) financially in the risks of product liability.

l) The manufacturers are aiming (persuade) the government (allow) them (use) the defence that reasonable steps (take) to withdraw the product when the hazard became known.

2. Complete the sentences below which give you practice in using certain frequently-used prepositional phrases.

a) We feel that, ... all costs, the law must be modified. If it is implemented, some companies will not be able to operate ...... a profit.

b) If someone injures himself ...... accident, the company can still, ... certain circumstances, be held liable.

c) ...... due course, we expect a huge increase in product liability lawsuits.

d) ...... average, since 1973, new product liability claims per firm in the US have totalled twelve.

e) ...... all probability, the EEC directive will become law.

f) The present law is, ... the whole, to the advantage of manufacturers.

g) The consumer associations are ...... no means sure their views will be accepted.

h) As ...... the size of awards, ... no account should it be assumed that these will be as large as in the States.

D Oral Work

1. Argue for or against the following debating theme:

'Imposing strict liability on manufacturers of products in EEC countries would place a totally unfair burden on them, and could act as a severe deterrent to innovation. The proposed legislation is against the interests of society as a whole.'

2. Discussion Topics

a) Is it fair that the mother of a 'thalidomide' baby should be generously compensated while the mother of a deformed baby, who has not taken the drug, should receive nothing from society?

b) Some people argue that government funds should be available to meet awards of compensation in excess of a certain fixed sum. In this way, governments would share in the risks of product liability and the producer's liability would be limited financially. What do you think of this proposal?

c) Some people say that an arbitrary period of limitation for product liability court actions would contradict the principle of strict liability. For example, a drug might only show its dangerous effects after ten or fifteen years. Comment on this view.

E Writing Exercises

1. Below, you are given part of the dialogue from a television programme about Product Liability. A representative of a Consumer Association is talking to an industrialist. Summarize the arguments of the two speakers. Use about 80–100 words.

Consumer
Representative: I know you always take the manufacturer's side, Malcolm, but the simple fact is that a company should take responsibility for the goods it makes, and it should be prepared to back its own judgement of what standard of safety is appropriate.

Industrialist: I agree to a certain extent with you, John. Certainly, a company should be expected to produce goods to a certain recognized standard or specification, and, if it fails to do so, it should be penalized. But remember, innovation is never without risk.......

Consumer
Representative: Well, surely that's what profits are all about; they're payment for risk-taking.

Industrialist: Yes, but producing new products is a service to society as a whole. However well tested a product is beforehand, one cannot predict possible dangers over a long time period, so the government should step in and help financially when someone is injured.

Consumer
Representative: Nonsense! Why should our tax be used to subsidize negligent companies. Businesses have simply got to assume the risks themselves, and make allowances, if necessary, in the prices they charge.

Industrialist: That means that prices will probably rise a great deal with products like pharmaceuticals, automotive parts, even toys perhaps.

Consumer
Representative: Possibly, but in most cases, insurance cover will be available and prices won't rise much. I'll bet you the consumer will hardly be affected at all, except in the high-risk areas you mentioned.

Industrialist: I still maintain we're going to get in Britain the kind of situation they now have in the US. Either companies will have to make their products so reliable that there's no chance of failure or they'll just have to get out of certain business areas altogether because insurance will be too costly.

Consumer
Representative: That's a gross exaggeration! We're not like the US for a start. We won't get the sort of explosion of product liability cases they've had. Compensation awards would not be as big over here, so fewer people will bother to take cases to court. Also, of course, the contingency fee system is not common in Britain. No, I'll say it again, British manufacturers must take responsibility for the goods they make, and they should leave the government out of it, by the way. We've got enough government interference as it is!

2. 'It is an acceptable defence for a manufacturer to say he took every reasonable precaution to manufacture a safe product, so he was not negligent, even if the product turned out to be dangerous or defective in fact.' Discuss this view.

Copyright — audio and video recording

Preparation

1. What does the term 'copyright' mean?
2. Why is it necessary?
3. In recent years the use of photocopiers, tape- and video-recorders has enormously increased. What effect would you expect this to have on the copyright protection given to such people as writers, musicians and artists?

Copyright protection is based on the moral principle of fair play. A person who works and produces something is entitled to own the product of his labour and skill. A copyright law, therefore, generally gives to an author, artist, or composer the right to prevent another
5 person copying an original work — a book, tune or picture — which he or she has created. This right to protection given to the creator of a work is found in copyright laws throughout the world and is also the basis of international conventions on the subject. Unfortunately, nowadays, this protection is being seriously threatened by modern
10 developments in the field of audio and video recording.

Whenever copyright laws come under review, investigating committees, when considering changes in the law, have to take into account certain facts of modern life. The first of these is that the tape recorder has become standard equipment in homes, libraries, schools
15 and other institutions. It is almost as indispensable as the radio and stereo; indeed, it is often incorporated with these in a single unit known familiarly as a 'music centre'. The video recorder, a much more expensive piece of equipment, is less widely used at present, but its price will steadily decrease and the number of users will grow.
20 This statement is substantiated by the declared intention of some powerful Japanese companies to commit substantial financial resources to developing their video recorder sales.

The increased use of tape- and video-recorders has created great problems for those who have to draft copyright laws which will be appropriate to modern conditions. It is now recognized that copyright in musical works and sound recordings is constantly infringed, everywhere.

Surveys have shown that when people are at home, they do not think twice about recording from the radio, and they have few scruples about copying commercial records and tapes borrowed from friends, music libraries and other such sources. Unauthorized recording has in fact become a national pastime in many countries. Furthermore, now that video recording is increasing, with the play-back equipment designed for use with TV sets, it is inevitable that film copyright will also come under attack.

The existence of widespread, unauthorized recording is undeniable. It is equally clear that, in a free country, it is impossible to check up on individuals who record in private and break copyright law. Policing such acts of infringement is really impractical. As a result, legal experts now find themselves in a dilemma. They operate on the principle that copyright owners must be protected by the law while, at the same time, they recognize that tape and video recording are making it difficult, if not impossible, for owners to exercise their legal rights.

How can composers, performers and the recording industry be given some income from recordings made privately at home or by libraries and other public institutions?

One approach to the tape recording problem has aroused great interest in international copyright circles. In West Germany they have opted for a levy system which is enforced by the German Copyright Act of 1965. This provides for a levy on a wide range of recording equipment in return for a blanket licence to make recordings in single copies for personal use. A maximum rate of 5% is laid down in the act.

This levy is imposed on all tape recorders suitable for making recordings of protected works for private use. Office dictating machines, large professional machines and the like are excluded. It is collected by a joint collecting society formed by three existing collecting societies representing composers, lyric writers, performers, record makers and other interested groups. In practice, apparently, the levy is not collected on a machine by machine basis but as a result of negotiation. The industry makes a lump sum payment each year to the joint collecting society on the basis of total sales.

Where recording equipment is combined with other equipment, e.g. a radio or 'Hi Fi' system, the levy is only calculated on the cost of the recording facility. The costs are in effect apportioned.

The German system, supported by many, has nevertheless had its critics. Some people say it is not a just system because it discriminates against buyers of tape recorders who have no intention of infringing copyright. Others argue that they should be able to record without paying additional remuneration to copyright owners.

The possibility of imposing a levy on blank tape has also been considered by West Germany and other nations. This kind of levy might reflect more accurately actual usage for recording, but it would involve a large operation by the authorities and possibly produce less revenue.

An illegal tape 'factory' in Hong Kong. The Preventive Service (customs) once had to hire two three-ton lorries to carry away some 70,000 tapes it seized in one raid.

If we wish to see what happens when copyright laws are largely ignored, we have only to look at areas in the Far East such as Hong Kong, Singapore, Malaysia and Taiwan — to name but a few. In most
80 Asian countries, the pirate cassette tape or record is big business. These countries are not only centres for the sale of such tapes but also bases for a multi-million dollar export trade in illegal recordings.

Piracy is probably most rampant in Hong Kong, so let us conclude this topic with a brief look at this area.
85 For every one legal cassette tape recording sold in Hong Kong, probably as many as thirty are sold illegally. The revenue from pirate tape sales greatly exceeds that from legitimate tape sales. When one takes into account the huge export trade in pirate recordings, some idea is gained of the extent of the business and of the fortunes being
90 made by racketeers. One recording industry executive in Hong Kong has been quoted as saying, 'the pirate tape industry has now reached epidemic proportions'.

The Hong Kong government has, in recent years, made determined efforts to stamp out this trade. In 1973, a special copyright
95 enforcement unit was set up to take over from the police. At about the same time, copyright offences came within criminal jurisdiction. The new enforcement unit tended to ignore the retailer of pirate tapes and to concentrate instead on the sources of these recordings. Intelligence networks were established. The co-operation of the
100 public was sought. Finally, numerous raids were carried out on pirate tape 'factories'. As a result, over 180 'pirates' have been convicted, fined and occasionally jailed, and of course, millions of dollars' worth of recording equipment seized.

Notwithstanding these efforts, business is still flourishing. After
105 all, profits are huge, setting up in business as a pirate is relatively easy, capital outlay on equipment is swiftly recouped, and penalties imposed by the courts are fairly lenient. Also, as one would expect, the pirates have become shrewder. They now store smaller numbers of tapes in any one place.
110 The recording companies are understandably concerned about illegal copying of tapes and records made by their highly paid

115 international stars. However, it is the Hong Kong local Chinese artistes who are most harmed by the pirate tape racket. Unlike international stars, they rely almost entirely on the local market for their income, and this comes mainly through tapes and records of their songs. How galling for them it must be when, perhaps a day or two after making a recording, they find that pirate tapes of it are on sale at knockdown prices in shops and stalls!

Language Notes

Line 21   *Commit financial resources to developing*. Note: 'to be committed to' is followed by the gerund ('ing') form, e.g. We are committed *to* spend*ing* more money on development projects.

Line 38   *Check up on*: watch/keep under surveillance, e.g. A jealous husband frequently checks up on his wife!

Line 52   *Blanket licence*: this term is explained in the writing exercise on page 108.

Line 82   *Multi-million dollar export trade*: the words 'million' and 'dollar' have no 's' endings because they are here used as adjectives.

A Comprehension

1. What justification is given in the text for the existence of copyright law?
2. In this modern, technological age, the legal expert who has to draft new copyright law is immediately faced by an obvious problem. Explain the nature of this difficulty.
3. What solution have the Germans found to the problem of widespread unauthorized recordings?
4. In what sense is the German system unfair to 'honest' buyers of tape-recorders?
5. What evidence is there in the text indicating that the pirate tape industry in Hong Kong is on a very large scale?
6. The efforts of the Hong Kong government to eliminate the illegal trade in pirate tapes have not been totally successful. Why is this so?

B Vocabulary

1. Supply words or phrases similar in meaning to those italicized in these sentences.

   a) In many homes, the tape-recorder is almost as *indispensable* as the TV.

   b) Copyright in sound recordings is constantly *infringed*.

   c) Most people have few *scruples* about copying commercial records.

   d) It is *inevitable* that film copyright will also be threatened.

103

e) *Policing* acts of infringement is virtually impossible.

f) Legal experts find themselves in a *dilemma*.

g) The Germans have *opted for* a levy system.

h) The recording equipment industry pays a *lump sum* to collecting societies.

i) Piracy of tapes is *rampant* in Hong Kong.

j) The government is determined to *stamp out* this practice.

k) Fortunes are being made by some *racketeers*.

l) Many *raids* are carried out by police on pirate factories.

m) The penalties for illegal taping are relatively *lenient*.

2. Interpretation of words and phrases. Circle the number next to the most appropriate answer.

a) The tape-recorder is often *incorporated* in what is known as a 'music centre'.
(i) fixed   (ii) added   (iii) combined

b) The Japanese companies will *commit* substantial resources to video sales.
(i) place   (ii) assign   (iii) find

c) Film copyright will soon *come under attack*.
(i) be threatened   (iii) become out-of-date
(ii) begin to disappear

d) The existence of widespread unauthorized recording is *undeniable*.
(i) indisputable   (ii) incredible   (iii) improbable

e) The levy *discriminates against* 'honest' buyers of tape-recorders.
(i) harms greatly   (iii) charges excessively
(ii) treats unfairly

f) The pirate tape industry in Hong Kong has reached *epidemic* proportions.
(i) vast   (ii) unforeseen   (iii) regrettable

g) 'Copyright offences came within criminal jurisdiction' means that:
(i) it became a criminal offence to break copyright.
(ii) it came into the jurisdiction of criminals.
(iii) it became a common crime to break copyright.

h) The purpose of the copyright enforcement unit in Hong Kong was:
(i) to try to get changes in copyright law
(ii) to search for retailers of pirate tapes
(iii) to try to find people who were breaking copyright law

i) The new enforcement unit tended to *ignore* the retailer of pirate tapes.
(i) be unaware of   (ii) take no notice of   (iii) neglect

j) *Intelligence networks* were established by the enforcement unit.
    (i) Well-organized sources of information
    (ii) Groups of highly intelligent workers
    (iii) Departments within the enforcement unit

k) *Notwithstanding* these efforts, business is *flourishing*.
    (i) As a result of   (i) booming
    (ii) Besides   (ii) improving
    (iii) In spite of   (iii) declining

l) Capital outlay is swiftly *recouped* by the pirate tape manufacturers.
    (i) recovered   (ii) spent   (iii) capitalized

m) The pirate tape manufacturers have now become *shrewder*.
    (i) more careful   (iii) more adventurous
    (ii) more astute

C Language Practice

1. Rewrite each sentence, replacing the italicized words or phrases with phrasal verbs chosen from the box below.
Example:
The British government will *introduce* a new copyright law.
The British government will **bring in** a new copyright law.

bring in
put up with
come up with
catch on
set up
take on
put off
turn out
crack down on
fall off
look into

a) Many companies have *delayed* signing international copyright agreements.

b) Because of illegal tape-recording, sales of records have *decreased* in recent years.

c) In some countries, the police *have dealt severely with* distributors of pirate tapes.

d) In parts of the Far East, artists have no option but to *tolerate* infringement of their copyright.

e) Songs which are 'hits' in Europe often *become popular* in Hong Kong and Singapore.

f) A committee to review copyright law was *established* in Britain in 1973.

g) This committee *produced* some very controversial recommendations.

h) An eminent judge *accepted* the job of acting as chairman.

i) The task of the committee *proved to be* long and complex.

j) The government is still *examining* ways of improving copyright law.

2. The exercise below gives further practice in the use of the definite and indefinite article. Indicate which, *if any*, should be used.

The problem of the photographic reproduction of [1]...... copyright works has been under [2]...... study at international level since at least 1961. The interest which [3]...... discussions have aroused reflects [4]...... almost universal desire to find [5]...... *modus vivendi* between, on the one hand, the legitimate copyright interests of [6]...... authors and publishers to control or at least receive [7]...... remuneration in respect of reproduction of their works and, on the other hand, [8]...... equally legitimate interests of those engaged in [9]...... research, in servicing research (for example, libraries) and [10]...... education who are mainly interested in [11]...... dissemination of information.

*Latin term meaning 'compromise' in this particular context.

D Oral Work

1. Argue for or against the following debating theme.

   'Sooner or later, copyright law in most countries will be as dead as the dodo.*'

   *A large *extinct* bird from Mauritius

2. Discussion Topics

   a) A government committee investigating copyright law in Britain visualized the following situation:

      'One can imagine a vicious circle. The increase in library and other copying will mean smaller circulations for books, journals, etc, which in turn means more copying. In the end, publication ceases — in some fields at least.'

      Do you think this situation could eventually arise in your own country? What can be done to prevent it?

   b) A person should be free to copy whatever tapes or records he wishes to. Comment on this view.

   c) In Britain, members of a committee examined copyright in relation to Industrial Design. They suggested two categories of design should be distinguished:

      Category A
      Designs which influence purchasing decisions (e.g. designs of wallpaper, cutlery, carpets, pottery, etc.) should be protected by copyright for twenty-five years from the time of marketing the article bearing the design. These articles would bear an internationally recognized copyright symbol.

      Category B
      This would include all shapes of three-dimensional objects where the appearance of the article did not influence the purchaser who 'buys the article only in the expectation that it will do the job for which it is intended.' Typical items in this category would be, for example, aircraft propellers or replacement parts in cars and other machinery to which no decorative additions had been made. This category would get *less* copyright protection.

      Discuss the value of this proposal.

E Writing Exercises

1. In Britain, a Committee of Inquiry investigated Copyright and Designs Law, and presented its findings in 1977. You are given below two extracts from the report the committee produced. The style of the paragraphs is *formal* as you would expect from an official government report.
   Instructions: summarize the content of each extract, using *simple, informal language*, as if you were telling a friend about the paragraphs in question. Each summary should be approximately one-quarter the length of the original paragraph.

   a) *Further Education*
      It was suggested to us* that the use of broadcast material for educational purposes in colleges of further education, training institutions, evening institutes and so on is, even more than in schools, dependent on its availability in recorded form. College timetables are so complex that the times of broadcasts seldom coincide with relevant class times; thousands of students attend on a part-time basis and are not in college or in class on the appropriate days, let alone at the exact times of broadcasts. Audio-visual equipment is usually concentrated in a particular place in the college where usually only technical staff can be available at the right time to make recordings for later use by teachers. We were told that the present conditions for recording are so restrictive as seriously to inhibit the use in further education of valuable broadcast material. Such use, it was suggested, can be encouraged only if the material can be made available at times appropriate to individual teachers and learning groups.

      *the Committee

   b) *Blanket Licensing*
      It is clear that different people have different ideas about what blanket licensing means, so this question will be considered first. Essentially, blanket licensing involves a group of copyright owners foregoing their rights to take individual action . . . in respect of the reprographic reproduction of their works. Instead of individual authors or publishers being responsible for collecting their own royalties, remuneration at a standard rate is collected by a central collecting agency or society which undertakes the task of distribution of the revenue to the individual copyright owners whose works are reproduced . . . From the user's point of view the essence of a blanket licence is that it covers all the works he wants to copy. For a single annual fee he gets permission to use any or all of the works in the licensor's repertoire. The Performing Right Society is a good example of a blanket licensing scheme in operation in the field of the public performance of music. The amount of the fee is based on the extent to which copyright works within the repertoire are likely to be used.

2. In your country, what effects is widespread use of photo-copying, audio- and video-recording having on such creative activities as writing, composing and designing?

National Stereotypes

Preparation

1. People often say such things as 'Italians are good lovers' or 'Englishmen are cold-blooded'. What other generalizations of this nature can you think of?
2. Do these generalizations serve any useful purpose? If so, what?
3. What do foreigners say about your own national character?

We are repeatedly warned to beware of generalizations yet, paradoxically, it seems that the human mind cannot resist categorizing people and things. We love to 'pigeon-hole', to make order out of a universe that frequently seems to us confusing and even chaotic. Nowhere is this tendency more evident that in our willingness to generalize about nationalities. We create national stereotypes and cling tenaciously to our prejudices. To illustrate this point, we shall take a look at the findings of a survey carried out by the market research firm, Parkland Research Europe.

This organization carried out a detailed study of European attitudes by questioning 185 business executives, lawyers, engineers, teachers and other professional people from seven European countries. These were: Germany; France; Britain; Switzerland; Italy; the Netherlands; Belgium. The resulting publication, *Guide to National Practices in Western Europe*, gave some idea of what Europeans think of each other. It revealed many widely-held stereotypes, but also came up with a few surprises. In the chart below, some of the data from this survey is summarized.

Parkland Findings

GERMANS	Liked themselves best of all. Most Europeans agreed that the Germans had the highest proportion of good qualities. They considered themselves very tolerant, but nobody else did. They saw themselves as fashionable. Others found them 'square'.
FRENCH	Not really admired by anyone except the Italians. Other Europeans found them conservative, withdrawn, chauvinistic, brilliant, superficial, hedonistic. Also, not very friendly. The French agreed on the last point!
BRITISH	Mixed reactions. Some found them calm, reserved, open-minded, trustworthy; others deemed them hidebound, insular and superior. Everyone was unanimous that the British had an excellent sense of humour. The British most admired the Dutch.

| | SWISS | Showed considerable lucidity and powers of self-analysis. Saw themselves as serious, trustworthy, but too money-minded and suspicious. Most Europeans agreed. The Swiss liked the Germans best. |
| 40 | | |

| | ITALIANS | Generally considered by everyone to be lazy and untrustworthy, and the Italians agreed! Most also found them to be vivacious, charming, hospitable and noisy. The Italians admired the French and the Dutch. Hardly anyone loved the Italians except the French. |
| 45 | | |

| | DUTCH | Most admired people in Europe — except by their neighbours — the Belgians. Everyone agreed that the Dutch are hard-working, thrifty, good-natured, tolerant and business-minded. The Netherlands, however, was not considered a good place to live in. |
| 50 | | |

| | BELGIANS | Least admired in this group. They see themselves as easy-going and diligent workers. Other Europeans consider them undisciplined and narrow-minded — and lousy drivers! |
| 55 | | |

As a follow-up to this study, businessmen were asked to imagine they were setting up a multinational company. They had to choose a
60   national for the positions of president, managing director, chief

109

cashier, public relations officer and skilled and unskilled labour.

The Germans came out of this exercise smelling of roses! They were universal choice for the top jobs, and also first choice for skilled workers. The Italians were relegated to the unskilled jobs; the French received massive support for the light-weight public relations post. According to the economist in charge of Parkland Research, 'No European picked an Italian as president or chief cashier. Moreover, no Italian or Frenchman picked one of his own nationals as chief cashier!'

What might have been the choices, one speculates, if *all* nationalities had been eligible for the above posts. Would the Japanese have swept the board? Surely not! Could a Japanese be chosen as chief cashier over a Swiss? And then, what about the Americans? They would surely force their way into the organization structure of this multinational company. And there again, there should be room for an industrious Chinese or a shrewd Russian ......

From theory, we turn to practice. We will conclude this topic by giving some examples of how national characteristics can affect business behaviour. We take as our source a study made recently by two British journalists of the problems encountered when Germans work in Britain and vice versa.

The German characteristics of industry and punctuality were illustrated by the example of a German executive who was appointed to the head of a specialist department of his company's branch in London. While he arrived at his office every morning on the dot, his senior employees rarely rolled up much before 10 a.m. For several weeks, harsh words were exchanged and tempers became more and more frayed. Finally, however, the German realized that his subordinates frequently worked on until eight or nine in the evening. They were doing certain work in the evening which he did early in the morning. Since most of the company's business was with the US, this kind of work schedule made sense. Eventually, the German changed his working hours — much to his wife's displeasure!

A British executive working in Germany found that he had to modify his employment policies because of the German liking for system and formality. He told the investigating reporters, 'A number of the German people we have employed have complained that we did not have a comprehensive enough policy manual.' He met the problem by spelling out in company recruitment advertising that employees had to have an understanding and liking for the British way of life. During interviews, he warned prospective employees that they would have to work in a much less formal environment than they were used to. Their colleagues would call them by their Christian names and expect this practice to be reciprocated. They would work on their own initiative and junior employees especially would probably have more responsibility than their counterparts in German companies.

Finally, the executive stressed that employees would be expected to make decisions based on a 'commonsense' interpretation of the company's policy guidelines rather than operate on the principle that 'if it's not in the book, it can't be done'.

The policy of this executive had certainly paid off since, with this approach to recruitment, staff turnover had been reduced significantly.

Language Notes

Line 2	*Paradoxically*: in a self-contradictory way/conflicting with what seems to us to be reasonable.
Line 2	*The human mind*: the article is used with a countable noun in this case to indicate *a whole class* — the minds of all human beings.
Line 5	*Nowhere is this tendency*: note the *inversion* of normal sentence order because the word 'nowhere' begins the sentence.
Line 7	*Prejudices*: irrational beliefs. A person is prejudiced *against* another person.
Line 10	*Carried out a detailed study*: a person *carries out* a study/survey/some research.
Line 18	*The data*: collective plural. We say: the data *was* significant.

A Comprehension

1. What reason is suggested by the author for our inherent tendency to generalize?
2. Which two words in paragraph 2 (l. 10–18) sum up what the Parkland survey was all about?
3. In the exercise involving the setting-up of a multinational company, which nationality appeared to do best and which worst? Give reasons for your answers.
4. The writer discusses the problem of a German executive working in London. Why was it sensible of this man's employees to work such unusual hours?
5. For what reason did the British executive in Germany have to modify his employment policies?
6. Summarize as briefly as possible the new approach the British executive had to use?

B Vocabulary

1. The colloquial and figurative expressions in this exercise are either in the text itself or could have been used in connection with it. Try to explain what each expression means.

   a) We love to *pigeon-hole* things.

   b) The report *came up with* a few surprises.

   c) The Germans came out of the exercise *smelling of roses*.

   d) He met the problem by *spelling out* that employees had to understand the British way of life.

   e) The policy of this executive has entirely *paid off*.

   f) Several people in the survey considered their countrymen to be *broad-minded*.

   g) The *big wheel* in our company is of German nationality.

h) When the employees *rolled up* at 10 a.m., the boss almost *hit the roof*.

i) German executives like to *go by the book*; British ones often prefer to *play it by ear*.

j) A friend of mine likes to entertain us by *doing take-offs* of different national types.

2. Tick (√) the word or phrase in each group which is closest in meaning to the one selected from the text.

Example: Repeatedly (l. 1)
                sometimes
                constantly √
                occasionally

a) Chaotic (l. 5)

    totally disordered
    rather frightening
    completely unintelligible

b) Tenaciously (l. 7)

    firmly
    blindly
    stupidly

c) Square
(German section)

    untidy
    tasteless
    conservative

d) Chauvinistic
(French section)

    excessively patriotic
    very arrogant
    too vain

e) Unanimous
(British section)

    certain
    convinced
    agreed

f) Vivacious
(Italian section)

    romantic
    talkative
    lively

g) Thrifty
(Dutch section)

    cheerful
    economical
    generous

h) Lousy
(Belgian section)

    average
    selfish
    bad

i) Relegated (l. 64)

    consigned to
    appointed to
    offered

j) Light-weight (l. 65)

    poorly-paid
    undemanding
    simple

k) Speculates (l. 70)

    wonders
    argues
    suggests

l) Shrewd (l. 76)

    profound
    astute
    tough

m) Frayed (l. 88)

    tired
    worn
    excited

n) Made sense (l. 92)

    was reasonable
    was profitable
    was economical

C Language Practice

1. Rewrite each of the groups of sentences as **one** sentence. Do not use *and*, *but*, *because* or *so*, but make any other necessary changes.

   a) We have just bought the Parkland guide. Now we can find out what Europeans think of each other.

   b) His employees turned up late every morning. He was furious with them. He decided to have a serious talk with them.

   c) I have two Swiss people staying at my house. I do not consider either of them to be money-minded. I do not find them excessively serious.

   d) Some Europeans consider the Italians to be dishonest. I recently visited Italy. I found them completely trustworthy.

   e) The British have their faults. They also have their qualities. They have an excellent sense of humour. They are famous for this throughout the world.

   f) I worked for a multinational based in Holland. I learned to admire the Dutch. I like their good nature and tolerance.

   g) We generalize about nationalities. When we do this, we often show prejudices. These are deeply-rooted in us. Their origins are obscure.

   h) We tried to pick nationalities for each post. We were obviously unfair to those we omitted. We were probably generous to some we selected.

2. Complete these sentences

   a) The Germans have a reputation ...... making good beer and the French are famous ...... their wine.

   b) The English take pleasure ...... talking about their bad weather. Indeed, they almost take pride ...... it.

   c) The Japanese show great respect ...... old people and are sensitive ...... their needs.

   d) Some people accuse the British ...... feeling superior ...... other nationalities.

   e) Many people are prejudiced ...... minority groups in their country.

   f) Some people are envious ...... the North American's standard of living.

   g) The Italians are said to be experts ...... making ice-cream.

   h) The Japanese are fond ...... eating raw fish and the French are mad ...... snails.

   i) The Italians are universally admired ...... their rich artistic tradition.

   j) A sense of humour is not peculiar ...... the British.

k) A passionate temperament is characteristic ...... Mediterranean people.

l) Ernest Hemingway, the American writer, believed the Spanish are obsessed ...... death.

D Oral Work

1. Argue for or against the following debating themes:

   a) 'By creating national stereotypes, we perpetuate racial disharmony.'

   b) 'The practice of making jokes at the expense of particular nationalities (e.g. Irish jokes or Polish jokes) is highly undesirable.'

2. Here are *five* subjects which are important to most human beings:

   Money   Business   Family   Love   Education

   Choose **one** group of nationalities from the list below, then compare and contrast the three nationalities you have chosen, limiting your comments to the topic areas given above:

   a) The Russians; the Chinese; the British

   b) The Japanese; the Indians (India); the Americans (USA)

   c) The French; the Italians; the Greeks

   d) The Germans; the Swedes; the Spanish

   e) The Saudi Arabians; the Iranians; the Brazilians

   f) The Australians; the British; the Canadians

   g) The Thais; the Indonesians; the Japanese

E Writing Exercises

1. Report assignment

   First of all, compose a chart showing which nationalities are represented in your class, and the numerical strength of each.
   When you have done this, interview *one* member of the class and find out what stereotyped impressions he or she has of the nationalities appearing in your chart.
   Finally, write a short report, including the chart, in which you will present the various attitudes held by your colleague. At the end of the report, comment on the impressions you have received.

2. Assuming that there is such a thing as 'a national character', write a critical analysis of the good and bad points of your own countrymen.

3. Choose a country you admire and analyze the character of its people.

Venezuela's Oil Revenues

Preparation

1. What problems might a government experience after nationalizing an oil industry previously run by foreign multinational organizations?
2. Venezuela, like other OPEC countries, is receiving huge revenues each year from the sale of its oil. What are some of the ways in which this wealth could be used? Are there, in your view, any obvious priority areas, common to most oil-producing countries, to which these revenues should be allocated?
3. What do the letters O.P.E.C. stand for? Which countries belong to this organization? What is the main aim of OPEC?

In 1976 the Venezuelan government took over all the foreign oil companies in the country, paid $1 billion in compensation, and placed the country's $5-billion industry under a holding company called Petróleos de Venezuela (Petroven). Almost overnight this new
5 state-owned enterprise made its entry on the world oil scene. Yet, to the surprise of many, it soon proved to be a roaring success, combining efficient management with imaginative marketing and distribution of its products.

The holding company, Petroven, employs some 24,000 employees.
10 It is managed almost entirely by Venezuelans. From the very beginning, it has steered clear of trouble. There have been no costly strikes; no shutdowns of plants. It has experienced none of the problems sometimes associated with nationalized industries in Latin America — bureaucratic slowness, financial losses, corruption,
15 featherbedding.

Petroven controls 14 operating companies (soon to be reduced to 5 or 6) which were former affiliates of foreign oil companies. To market its oil outside Venezuela, the government uses the services of the big multinationals such as Exxon and Shell. These provide technological
20 and marketing knowhow under contract.

Petroven's most important customers are the US (which takes about 35% of Venezuela's oil exports), Canada and the Caribbean countries. It has also successfully used its marketing expertise to build up sales to non-traditional clients, who now account for 20% of oil exports.
25 These new customers, about 50 in all, are generally final users rather than oil companies or traders. They are, for example, power authorities, small refineries and government organizations.

In approaching new customers, Petroven has one important advantage. It can offer a much wider range of crude oils and refined
30 products than most Middle East oil producers.

The country's oil revenues make a big contribution to the government's income. In its first 18 month's of operation, Petroven collected about $14 billion for sales of crude oil, refined products and natural gas. It paid the government taxes and royalties of about $10
35 billion. The sum represented about 70% of the state's ordinary income.

Derricks sprout everywhere out of
oil-rich Lake Maracaito, Venezuela.
The Creole Petroleum Corporation
maintain a fleet of 400 boats to ferry
personnel and link up their hundreds
of oilwells on the lake.   40

These revenues will continue for many years to come. Admittedly,
the level of proven reserves is diminishing. In fact, the country may
not be able to continue producing 2.2 million barrels a day up to the
end of the century. However, it has huge 'probable reserves' locked
up in the Orinoco Tar belt in the south. These are perhaps seven
times as great as the amount of proven reserves, but they may be
difficult to extract and refine because of their high tar content. Also,
there is an ongoing programme of oil exploration. No doubt, new
45 fields will be discovered in due course.

Venezuela, in common with other oil producers, faces the challenge
of how best to spend its revenues in the interests of the country.

Its answer has been to work out an ambitious programme of
spending on industrial and social development. This Fifth National
50 Plan provided for massive government spending between 1976–1980
although all the projects probably will not be completed until 1982 or
1983. Its main aim is to reduce the country's dependence on oil
revenues, and to diversify the economy by strengthening the
industrial and agricultural sectors. A second objective is to
55 redistribute national wealth by creating hundreds of thousands of
new jobs.

This programme will involve public and private investment in the
region of $52 billion — a lot of money to spend on 12 million people
in a short time.

60 In this country, the state participates heavily in the economy. Some
say the Venezuelan government has a 'finger in every pie'. Because of
its dominating role, much of the spending is being done by the
government. It is investing in the steel, aluminium, hydro-electric
and nuclear power industries; it is also putting money into social
65 welfare programmes. Finally, by using various incentives, for

example cheap credit, it is trying to channel private investment into such areas as agriculture, tourism and light industry.

Venezuela has found that elaborate development programmes bring plenty of problems. Like Saudi Arabia and Nigeria, its ports
70 have struggled to cope with the volume of imported goods. Bottlenecks in supplies have occurred. Costs have risen. Building materials, especially, have been in short supply.

The major problem has been that there are not enough trained and skilled personnel to carry out all these projects. The government is
75 now pulling out all the stops to remedy the situation. It is offering comprehensive training programmes at Venezuelan universities and technical colleges; it has a scholarship scheme which supports thousands of Venezuelans studying overseas; it has signed an agreement with a European inter-governmental organization, the
80 purpose of which is to encourage skilled workers, technicians and professional people to work in Venezuela. It is also making local companies train specified numbers of new apprentices.

Another problem is that the country's domestic consumption of petrol has been increasing at an alarming rate. However, in order to
85 control inflation, the government has been selling petrol at prices the President calls 'the lowest in the world'. It is doubtful that Venezuela can continue to invest millions of dollars in refining capacity, only for the petrol to be sold to its people at prices below production cost.

A question people are asking is: 'Will the country's commitments
90 to costly projects put too great a pressure on its resources? Has the government, in fact, bitten off more than it can chew?'

The key to Venezuela's future prosperity is its oil industry. Provided this remains competitive, there seems no reason why development cannot be sustained. And why should one doubt Petroven's abilities?
95 It is run professionally and has an excellent track record. Obviously, the programme may be implemented at a slower pace; some rephasing may be necessary. But the plan should not be prohibitively expensive. After all, in five or ten years time, certain industries like steel and aluminium should be producing enough for the import bill
100 of these goods to be reduced.

In years to come, we will be able to judge how well the government has used the oil revenues. Some will measure success by looking at how the country has broadened and strengthened its industrial bases. Others will look to see if it has become a more egalitarian society.
105 Venezuela has the highest per capita income in Latin America, but its wealth is unevenly distributed. There are rich people in Caracas who will pay $100,000 to join the Country Club, but there are large numbers of urban poor, some living in shanty towns.

An intriguing question is: will Venezuela achieve real social and
110 economic progress with its five-year plan, or will the country end up with massive debts and lost illusions?

Behind the towering monuments of modern architecture, Caracas is a maze of *ranchitos*, the cardboard shanty towns.

Language Notes

Line 11	*Steered clear of*: avoided
Line 12	*Shutdown*: a temporary closing of a plant
Line 108	*Shanty towns*: towns where poor people live, mostly in huts and makeshift dwellings
Line 109	*Intriguing*: very interesting

A Comprehension

1. How do you think most Venezuelans feel now about their government's decision to nationalize the oil industry? Give reasons for your answer.
2. What kind of business relationship does the Venezuelan government now have with the foreign oil companies?
3. What is an unusual feature of Petroven's overseas sales?
4. The level of Venezuela's proven oil reserves is diminishing. How serious a problem is this for the country?
5. In what way will Venezuela's economy and society be changed by the government's five-year development plan?
6. What could be a major obstacle to the realization of the government's projects?
7. Explain why the low price of petrol is not necessarily in Venezuela's interests?
8. The five-year plan is ambitious and will be extremely costly to complete. In the writer's view, what are the chances of its being carried out successfully?

B Vocabulary

1. Find words or phrases in the text (l. 1–55) which mean these things:
    a) Organization controlling the shares of subsidiaries.
    b) Achieving excellent results.
    c) Avoided difficulties.
    d) Supporting inefficient enterprises.
    e) Organizations linked to but not wholly owned by the parent company.
    f) Specialized knowledge of selling.
    g) Unrefined.
    h) Stocks of oil already discovered.
    i) Get out of the ground.
    j) Continuing.
    k) After some time has passed; in the near future.
    l) A demanding task.
    m) Put into effect.
    n) Change the economic structure of a country/broaden its industrial base.

2. Interpretation of words and phrases. Circle the number next to the most suitable answer.

    a) The new customers of Petroven are generally *final users*. These want the oil to:
       (i) distribute to big companies.
       (ii) use for their own purposes.
       (iii) sell again on international markets.

b) The government is trying to *channel* private investment into such areas as agriculture and tourism.
(i) direct   (ii) subsidize   (iii) force

c) Its ports have *struggled to* cope with the volume of imported goods.
  (i) made efforts to
  (ii) used special methods to
(iii) looked for ways to

d) The government cannot continue to invest millions of dollars in oil-refining *capacity*.
(i) equipment   (ii) processes   (iii) facilities

e) Will the country's *commitments* put pressure on its resources?
  (i) what it is thinking of financing
  (ii) what it has undertaken to carry out
(iii) what it now has under consideration

f) Petroven has *an excellent track record*. The writer is referring to:
  (i) the past performance of the enterprise.
  (ii) the excellent financial situation of the company.
(iii) the good prospects for the organization.

g) Some *rephasing* of the programme may be necessary.
  (i) dropping some projects which are too expensive
  (ii) reshaping of the programmes to achieve economies
(iii) changing the times when certain projects will be carried out

h) The programme should not be *prohibitively expensive*.
  (i) so expensive that it brings disaster.
  (ii) too costly to be run efficiently.
(iii) so costly that it cannot be realized.

3. These idiomatic expressions are either in the text or have been used by people when referring to the topic. Try to explain what each phrase means.

a) Some years before the oil was nationalized, the foreign companies *saw the writing on the wall* and slowed down their investment.

b) The government is *pulling out all the stops* to increase the number of trained personnel.

c) Has the Venezuelan government *bitten off more than it can chew*?

d) Venezuela still presents the image of a country *riding the crest of a petroleum boom*.

e) The five-year plan is *a blueprint* for national development.

f) Like the Venezuelans, the British have now discovered oil and they are wondering what to do with this *bonanza*.

g) Venezuela has had a dispute with the foreign multinationals regarding unpaid tax. The oil executives are *keeping a low profile*, hoping that the fuss will die down.

C Language Practice

1. Choose a suitable word or phrase from the box below to link each pair of sentences. Make any other necessary changes.

   Example: The plan should be completed. It may take longer than expected.
   — The plan should be completed. **However**, it may take longer than expected.

However
thus
on the contrary
yet
nor
regardless of
despite
with a view to
while
on the other hand
accordingly
as well as
moreover

   a) There is a lack of skilled personnel. The government has introduced manpower training schemes.

   b) Exploration is now being carried out. Its purpose is to discover new reserves of oil.

   c) The state oil company is beginning a big new programme of exploration. We can expect new finds to be announced in due course.

   d) The government will press on with its projects. Criticisms of the opposition parties will not affect its plans.

   e) Venezuela is receiving vast revenues. It may still have to borrow heavily to finance its schemes.

   f) It is one of the richest Latin American countries. It is one of the most democratic.

   g) Petroven has been a commercial success. The predictions of foreigners were extremely gloomy.

   h) The state oil company has not made any serious mistakes. It has, in fact, adopted wise management and marketing policies.

   i) Venezuela is a very prosperous country. Its people are free and contented.

   j) You can find poverty in Caracas. There are also areas of great wealth.

   k) The country does not have enough middle-management personnel. It also does not have enough technicians.

   l) Some OPEC leaders criticize countries for wasting fuel. Oil consumption in their own countries is often extremely high.

2. Write sentences which are similar in meaning to those below. Use the sentence openings provided and make any necessary changes.

   a) Petroven is in a favourable position because it can offer a wide range of crude oils.
   One advantage ......

   b) According to some people, the country may not be able to continue producing 2.2 million barrels a day.
   Some people question ......

   c) The main aim of the government is to reduce the country's reliance on oil revenues.
   The government wants to make ......

d) The government is investing large sums in high-priority industries and putting money into social welfare programmes.
Not only ......

e) There have been price controls on a wide assortment of consumer goods, yet inflation has continued.
Inflation has continued despite ......

f) Technical staff have been lacking, so the government has not been able to meet all the targets in its plan.
The lack of technical staff ......

g) 'Even if the oil dries up next year, the foreign banks will never desert Venezuela. They have an investment here', an economist said.
An economist argued ......

h) Like other members of OPEC who have implemented ambitious programmes, Venezuela has had to face many problems.
Venezuela is similar ......

i) If it is to prosper economically, Venezuela must handle its limited reserves with care.
Venezuela's industrial prosperity depends ......

D Oral Work

1. Discussion Topics

a) 'Oil is power.' Discuss this statement with reference to the oil-producing countries of the Middle East.

b) 'Future historians, looking back on our century, may well take the view that oil was a curse, rather than a blessing, to mankind.' Discuss.

c) Many oil-producing countries have such vast revenues from oil that they cannot use these up on projects for their own people. What should these countries do with the surplus revenues at their disposal?

E Writing Exercises

1. Some experts believe that known reserves of oil could be exhausted by the first half of the 21st century. They also predict that world demand for energy will outstrip supplies by the end of this century. What steps, in your view, should be taken to avoid a future world energy crisis?

2. Outline some of the problems which arise when a relatively undeveloped country — in economic terms — begins to receive revenues from the sale of its oil. Support your views with as many examples as possible.

3. 'Because of a shortage of energy supplies, the living standards of the industrialized countries are likely to decline in the years to come'. Discuss.

EEC Industrial Policy — what do you do with 'lame ducks'?

Preparation

1. What is the European Economic Community? Which nations belong to it? What are some of its aims?
2. In the EEC countries there are certain large companies, and even industries, which are known as 'lame ducks'. Can you define the term or guess what it means?
3. In what business activities or industrial projects might co-operation between EEC members be beneficial?
4. Why do you think co-operation between EEC members — mergers of European companies, joint ventures, manufacturing agreements, etc — has so often failed?

The industrial policy of the EEC is based on the principle of equal, competitive conditions between enterprises, the removal of barriers to trade between member countries, and the destruction of cartel agreements or other restrictive business practices of this type. There are, nevertheless, certain sectors of industry where this policy cannot be applied, and where cartels or protectionist measures have had to be set up.

The Industrial Policy department of the EEC's Commission has recognized that certain science-based industries should be treated as

10 special cases. Among these are the computer, nuclear energy, aircraft and telecommunications industries. In this sector, national markets are too small to provide a viable base for the industries. Obviously it makes sense to develop them on a European level and with inter-governmental co-operation. Usually national governments are

15 the big customers in these markets, and it is they who provide most of the money for research and development. These industries, by their nature, remain to some extent outside the market economy.

A second group that receives special treatment from the EEC is composed of what we might term 'problem industries'. The survival

20 of these would be threatened if preventive action were not taken. They are all in major structural crises. They cannot pay their way in the market but they are too important to the countries concerned to be allowed to die. They need to readjust to changed circumstances in their industrial sector, so that later, when they are healthier, they can

25 start paying their way again in the Community.

These weak, threatened industries are sometimes called 'lame ducks'. In the EEC they include the steel, synthetic fibres, shipbuilding, textile and paper industries. The EEC has had to take an active part in trying to solve their problems. It refers to its efforts

30 as 'crisis action'. Take the case of steel. Practically every large steel firm in the EEC is in serious financial difficulty, some are technically bankrupt. There is a massive world surplus of capacity which will probably continue for years. As much as 15% of the EEC workforce in the industry faces the threat of redundancy.

35   The EEC's strategy in this case has been to allow a 'crisis cartel'.
This will enable the industry to restructure and rationalize, protected
obstacles   by import barriers and price regulations. Community money has
been made available to members so that they can modernize their
plants. It will also be used to ease the burden of redundancy   *alleviate*
40   payments. The main aim of setting up the cartel was to slim the
industry down to a more viable size. In this case the Community has
been successful in getting firms to accept its approach.
        In the case of the synthetic fibres industry, the Commission has
also got broad acceptance for its policies. For example, it asked
45   governments not to aid capacity expansion for the next two years,
agreed   and they complied with the request. It also asked 13 major companies
in the European markets to freeze their capacity levels. All but the
Italians agreed to do this.
        One can have some sympathy with the Italian point of view. After
50   all, they had spent a great deal of money in recent years,
re-equipping and modernizing their synthetics industry. They did
not want to lose the opportunity to get a larger share of the market.
        The paper, shipbuilding and textile industries are in no better
shape than steel and synthetic fibres. Soon, without doubt, the EEC
55   will start taking crisis action with them. Already, in fact, in the early
1970s, the Director-General of Industrial Policy at that time made
attempt   efforts to rationalize the shipbuilding industry.
        It is a reflection of the great structural crises through which many
European industries are passing that it is the EEC, traditionally so   *customarily*
60   opposed to cartels, which is now proposing such practices in order to
stabilize prices and trade in certain sectors.
        Some people believe that if the EEC succeeds with its crisis action
approach, it should begin playing a part in other sectors of industry.
It could help to restructure and strengthen certain industries so that
65   they could meet the challenge of US and Japanese competition in
some of the tougher markets.
        There are experts who argue that, in the automobile market,   *reason*
co-operation between major European companies will be crucial to   *critical /*
the survival of an EEC car industry. By the mid 1980s, they predict,   *vital*
70   the Americans and the Japanese will dominate the small and medium
car markets, with strong competition also coming from the Russians
and Koreans. Even the Brazilians and the Spanish will be getting into
the act.
        To meet such challenges, the experts say that EEC car makers will
75   have to pool their resources to survive. They will have to co-operate
on standardizing their car designs and also in manufacturing.
Particularly   Especially, they will be forced to combine on research instead of, as
wasting   now, dissipating their money, time and expertise by competing
against each other. Because their market will have shrunk, they will
80   have to design and build Eurocars. To support their views, the
experts point to recent developments in co-operation, such as British
Leyland and Renault agreeing to share technical knowledge, or the
Renault/Peugeot/Volvo co-operation on engine development and
manufacture.
85   It is certain that further European integration is needed in some
industries, e.g. aerospace and computers, but governments often find
it difficult to co-operate with each other, so the record of European
co-operation in industry is rather poor. The Anglo-French Concorde

was a costly failure, and Britain pulled out of the Franco-German
airbus project. In the computer industry, France entered into a joint
venture with Philips of Holland and Siemens of West Germany, but
the project failed. The French have preferred to create a large national
corporation in this key industry, and they have now formed a
partnership with the US computer concern, Honeywell.

In industries where heavy research and development costs are
involved, the Community policy has been to try to broaden the
market and maximize the returns for the companies concerned. In the
European telecommunications industry, for instance, the
Commission did not intervene directly, but it promoted discussion
between Europe's national PTT (Post, Telephones and
Telecommunications) authorities on harmonizing future technology,
and it persuaded them to look outside their own countries before
deciding what to buy.

Many support the EEC policy towards lame ducks, since they feel
that, if major restructuring of industries has to be done, then it
should be handled at European level by the EEC, which is, after all,
dedicated to the ideal of free competition. However, there are many
people who do not wish Brussels to intervene in sectors where there
is no immediate crisis; nor do such people think the EEC authorities
should engage in the practice of backing 'winners', i.e. giving funds
to strengthen certain enterprises, or encouraging mergers to create
powerful transnational organizations which can compete better in the
harsh competitive world. As one official has said, 'It is no business of
civil servants to go picking winners either between sectors of
industry or between products'. In other words, the EEC should not
put itself in the place of Europe's industrialists.

Because of this kind of attitude, it will remain difficult to achieve a
great deal of co-operation at government level. Even the 'European
technological community '— composed of supra-national
science-based industries — which had once seemed feasible, now
appears to be something of a pipe dream.

Language Notes

Line 26   *These weak, threatened industries*: a useful synonym
                 for 'weak' is 'vulnerable'. In most countries there
                 are certain industries which are vulnerable to
                 foreign competition.

Line 32   *bankrupt*: be careful when using this word. Here are some examples of correct usage:
a) Our firm is bankrupt/It is a bankrupt firm.
b) Last month, many companies went bankrupt.
c) The bankruptcy of a large firm is usually commented on in the press.

Line 32   *capacity*: production capability. When a concern is working below capacity, its production facilities are not being fully utilized. Most companies would like their plants to be working to full capacity.

Line 34   *workforce*: total number of workers in an organization. We could also say 'staff', 'personnel' or 'employees'.

Line 36   *rationalize*: to 'rationalize' a company or industry means to reorganize it in order to make it more efficient and competitive.

Line 37   *Community money*: funds provided by EEC institutions.

Line 80   *To support their views*. Instead of 'support', we could say 'back up'.

A Comprehension

1. In the text, the writer groups together (l. 10) the computer, nuclear energy, aircraft and telecommunications industries. Why does he think these should be treated differently from most other industries?
2. Explain why the steel industry is a good example of a 'lame duck'.
3. What is 'crisis action'? When is such action necessary?
4. To what extent was the EEC's policy of 'crisis action' successful in the case of the synthetic fibres industry?
5. Summarize briefly the main arguments for the EEC intervening in industries which are *not* experiencing any real difficulties or problems.
6. What prospects does the writer see for future co-operation between EEC countries in the industrial field?

B Vocabulary

1. Paraphrase each sentence so as to show clearly the meaning of the words in *italics*.

   Example: The EEC Commission considers the nuclear energy industry *a special case*.
   — *The EEC Commission treats the nuclear energy industry differently from many other industries*.

   a) Some industries *cannot pay their way in the market*.

   b) There will be a *world surplus of steel capacity* for many years to come.

   c) Most European steel industries are *technically bankrupt*.

d) Community money will *ease the burden of redundancy payments*.

e) It is hoped the industry will be *reduced to a more viable size*.

f) Thirteen synthetic fibres companies have been asked to *freeze their capacity levels*.

g) Co-operation between European car manufacturers is *crucial to the survival of an EEC car industry*.

h) The EEC car makers will have to *pool their resources to survive*.

i) The idea of a European technological community now appears to be *something of a pipe dream*.

2. Complete each sentence using an appropriate form of the word in *italics*.

a) *industrial* The ...... of a country is often accompanied by unexpected problems.

b) *destruction* Our chairman is almost 95 years old. He seems almost ....

c) *type* A lack of capital is ...... of small companies.

d) *recognize* Her promotion was in ...... of her services to the company.

e) *special* Although ...... in finance, she also is very knowledgeable about the technology of our industry.

f) *solve* We have worked unsuccessfully on the problem for months. It appears to be ....

g) *ease* The Minister of Finance announced that there would be no ...... of credit restrictions in the near future.

h) *viable* Because of increased costs, many people are now questioning the ...... of the whole project.

i) *strategy* Nuclear energy is an industry of ...... importance in our economy.

j) *large* We can easily ...... our factory since we own all the surrounding land.

k) *sympathy* The bank manager agreed to treat my request for a loan ....

l) *stable* ...... a currency's rate of exchange can sometimes be a very difficult job for a finance minister.

m) *predict* He used to be cheerful, but since his illness, his mood has been very ....

n) *survive* The ...... of firms in bad times often depends on efficient management.

o) *intervene* When neither side in a labour dispute will give way, the ...... of an independent arbitrator is often necessary.

p) *feasible*   We have called in a firm of engineering consultants to carry out a ...... study.

3. Interpreting words and phrases. Circle the number next to the most suitable answer.

   a) *Cartel agreements* (l. 6) generally result when:
      (i) a group of companies decides to share a market to avoid competition.
      (ii) one company is dominating the market and excluding all competition.
      (iii) a large number of firms are making excessive profits in an industry.

   b) Industries *in major structural crises* (l. 21):
      (i) should be encouraged to expand their production facilities.
      (ii) ought to be managed by some kind of state agency.
      (iii) need to reorganize and adapt to market conditions.

   c) Even the Brazilians and Spanish will be *getting into the act*. (l.72):
      (i) achieving a high level of car exports.
      (ii) obtaining a share of the car market.
      (iii) co-operating with other car manufacturers.

   d) If EEC manufacturers co-operate *on standardizing their car designs* (l.75):
      (i) there will probably be fewer car models produced by EEC manufacturers.
      (ii) there will probably be higher standards in the car industry.
      (iii) there will probably be an increase in the number of car designs by EEC manufacturers.

   e) The phrase *backing winners* (l. 110) refers to:
      (i) attempts by EEC officials to make certain companies or industries more competitive.
      (ii) support given by governments to 'lame duck' industries.
      (iii) efforts by industrialists to win back export markets.

C Language Practice

1. Use each of the words in the given order to form meaningful sentences.

   Example: EEC/dedicated/ideal/free competition/member countries.
                 — *The EEC is dedicated to the ideal of free competition among member countries.*

   a) Nuclear energy/industry/developed/co-operation/European governments.

   b) Science-based industries/special cases/national markets/too small/developed profitably.

    c) Problem industries/only survive/EEC/intervenes/protect/tariff barriers.

    d) Many people believe/essential/European car manufacturers/co-operate/challenge/US and Japanese competitors.

    e) Many examples prove/EEC members/difficult/co-operate/joint industrial projects.

    f) Debatable/EEC/support/industries/sound financial position.

2. Complete the passage below using any appropriate word for each blank space.

> Since[1] ...... EEC has a policy for steel and shipbuilding, should it also have[2] ...... for the car industry? This question is frequently brought[3] ...... in the conversation of European motor manufacturers. The [4]...... Director of Fiat argues that the European car industry must regroup and reorganize if it is to stand[5] ...... to the challenge of Japanese vehicle manufacturers. Since Europe is[6] ...... attack from Japanese vehicle imports, especially of [7]...... and small commercial vehicles, he thinks that the EEC countries should not put [8]...... barriers against [9]...... Japanese. The EEC should resist the tendency [10]...... protectionism. Instead, EEC manufacturers should work [11]...... a common policy [12]...... dealing with their problems. They should conduct research [13]...... methods of achieving larger scale economies of production. Many people in the car industry [14]...... this view. They are worried [15]...... the alarming increase [16]...... Japanese car exports to Europe. They cannot see a European car industry [17]...... into the 21st century without some kind of [18]...... by the EEC authorities.

D Oral Work

1. Argue for or against the following debating theme: 'In general, governments are extremely unwise to support "lame duck" companies. In the long run such support is usually extremely expensive, unprofitable, and sometimes even disastrous.'

2. Discussion Topics

    a) In the case of the European car industry, would it be better if the EEC authorities intervened to ensure better use of resources, for example by encouraging mergers, joint projects and rationalization of the industry, or should such steps only be taken on the initiative of the car manufacturers themselves?

    b) What might be some of the advantages and disadvantages of 'Eurocars'?

    c) Do you have any 'lame duck' companies or industries in your country? What kind of help or protection is being given to them?

E Writing Exercises

1. Below, you will find an incomplete dialogue between the Chief
   Executive of a British car manufacturer, Mr Joseph H., and his
   counterpart in an Italian company, Signor Carlo G.
   Where you find gaps in the dialogue, write down what you think
   the speakers probably said.

   J.H.: What I've been trying to say to you for the last hour, Carlo,
   is that our companies should co-operate more.

   C.G.: ......

   J.H.: Well, what have I got to do to convince you?

   C.G.: ......

   J.H.: OK, take automatic gearboxes. Neither of us uses enough at
   the moment to justify the money we're putting into making
   them.

   C.G.: ......

   J.H.: Exactly. Both of us would save money if we did that.

   C.G.: Yes, we could also take a look at other components —
   engines, for example.

   J.H.: ......

   C.G.: Oh, come on now. It shouldn't be too difficult. We could set
   up a common engine plant.

   J.H.: ......

   C.G.: Either in Britain or Italy. Anyway, who would ever know
   whether the engine had been made in a British or Italian
   plant?

   J.H.: ......

   C.G.: Oh, you're exaggerating, Joseph. I honestly believe the
   British worker is as industrious and skilled as any in
   Europe.

   J.H.: ......

   C.G.: I haven't touched a drop all day. In any case, I hate scotch!

   J.H.: I'm just joking! Anyway, how about continuing our chat in
   the bar?

   C.G.: ......

   J.H.: Certainly not. While you're in England, you're *my* guest.

2. Essay topic: discuss ways in which your country co-operates or
   could co-operate with other countries in the industrial field.

3. Summarize the section of the topic which begins on line 8, and
   which ends on line 43.
   Write your summary using 60–80 words.

Women Directors in the USA

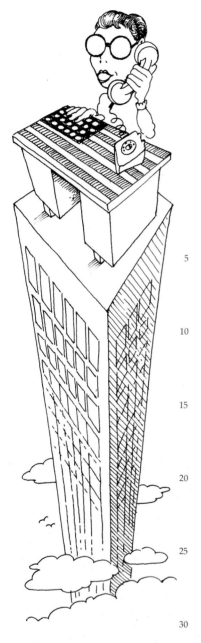

Preparation

1. In which countries of the world is it now possible, and increasingly common, for women to 'get to the top' in the business world? Can you name countries where it is virtually impossible for them to do this?
2. What factors make it easier and more common in some countries for women to become directors of companies?
3. What qualities can help a woman to reach a top management position? Are these qualities the same as those a man would need?

When Juanita Kreps was made the first woman Secretary of Commerce in the USA and Patricia Harris the second woman Secretary of Commerce and Urban Development, the accompanying publicity revealed that they held nine directorships, and what is

5   more, these were of eminent corporations or organizations such as the New York Stock Exchange, Eastman Kodak, Chase Manhattan and International Business Machines. The high status and considerable power in the business world of these two women highlighted the fact that women directors are becoming more and more common in the

10   US. In 1970 there was scarcely a handful, mostly female relatives of corporate founders; now the number exceeds 400, and is steadily growing.

    It is generally conceded that most of today's women directors are able women bringing expertise and business acumen to their jobs.

15   This is not surprising. Most women now old enough to serve on boards had to fight their way up the corporate ladder. They had to be not only equal, but better than their male colleagues, in order to survive.

    The advantage of women directors is that they can serve as

20   women's representatives. This is important to US companies, which are increasingly sensitive to women's place in business, and are groping for ways to deal with it. Nevertheless, not all women directors see their role in this light. One well-known woman has confessed that she disliked the idea of 'special interest directors'. 'I

25   don't feel I should represent the woman's point of view', she said. She believed she represented the stockholders and the public.

    Yet, even this woman was forced to admit that she played a 'kind of consciousness-raising role' on her boards. She found herself pointing out to board members, for example, that as more women

30   worked, the number of valuable people unwilling to uproot themselves would increase. Therefore, corporations would have to change the environment in which they hired, trained and promoted employees.

    Women have commented on aspects of their roles as women

35   directors. Juanita Kreps remarked that since she represented women she had to prepare extra carefully for board meetings so that 'I won't ruin other women's chances to enjoy the same opportunity'.

Jane Pfeiffer, who was IBM's first woman vice-president, considered that an important function of the woman director was to increase corporate awareness of women's status. For instance, in discussing executive resources, she would say, 'When are we going to have a woman at that level?' and start talking about possible candidates. Often, a male director brought up the subject, but if he did not, she certainly would!

Many women agreed that their presence on a board acted as a kind of pressure on other members and management as a whole. Because a woman is on the board, it automatically gets reports on women's issues and executives know that such reports will receive sharp scrutiny by at least one board member.

An important advantage of women directors, it is claimed, is that they can take a different perspective from male directors — an outside view. Male directors tend to eat at the same club and mingle with other corporate executives. Women are usually more involved with family relationships, buying for the home, the education of children, volunteer activities and so on; they can take a different view from men who tend to become exclusively involved with their work life.

Patricia Harris believes that women are willing to look beyond 'the normal sources of talent and respectable information' when they function as directors. They can take a fresh approach to problems. 'People who have always been in the power orbit . . . tend to get blinders', she says.

What about women directors' relations with their colleagues? We may quote Juanita Kreps regarding this. 'Once I was on the board, I have never had any difficulty being accepted. I feel I am on a completely equal footing with the other members, and my suggestions get whatever consideration they deserve on their merits'.

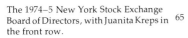
The 1974–5 New York Stock Exchange Board of Directors, with Juanita Kreps in the front row.

Some women directors are willing to acknowledge that they owe their directorships to their sex in the sense that there was the initial decision to include a woman on the board. To this extent they are
70 symbols of corporate response to social change, as well as being working directors, of course.

Today, the 400 or so women directors represent only 2.7% of the 15,000 directorships of major corporations. It may be many years before women's presence will make a significant impact upon boardroom
75 decisions, but that time will surely come.

Language Notes

Line 32   *Hired*: workers are 'hired'; 'employed'; 'taken on'. They may, if they are unlucky, be 'fired'; 'dismissed' or, in colloquial language, 'sacked'; 'kicked out' of a company.

Line 61   *Blinders*: North American term for 'blinker': literally, a screen to prevent a horse from seeing sideways.

A Comprehension

1. What interesting information was learned by the public when Juanita Kreps and Patricia Harris were appointed to their government posts?
2. Why is it not surprising that women directors in the US are generally very able?
3. For what reason are many US companies only too glad to have a woman director on their board?
4. One woman said she played a 'kind of consciousness-raising role' (l. 28). What did she mean?
5. In what sense, according to the text, is it possible that women might be more 'objective' in their business life?
6. Women directors are 'symbols of corporate response to social change' (l. 70). Explain the meaning of this statement.
7. To what extent does the author come to any kind of conclusion regarding future prospects for women directors in the US?

B Vocabulary

1. Tick (√) the word or phrase in each group which is closest in meaning to the one selected from the text.
   Example: Revealed (l. 4)
                          told
                          disclosed √
                          mentioned

   a) Eminent (l. 5)   b) Status (l. 7)
       large   reputation
       powerful   position
       distinguished   ability

c) Highlighted (l. 8)

emphasized
concealed
overlooked

d) Conceded (l. 13)

admitted
argued
agreed

e) Acumen (l. 14)

knowledge
experience
discernment

f) Corporate ladder (l. 16)

the ranks of the company
the promotion prospects
the managerial positions

g) Groping (l. 22)

searching
waiting
hoping

h) Uproot themselves (l. 30)

co-operate
move
disrupt

i) Sharp scrutiny (l. 48)

close examination
further investigation
careful criticism

j) Mingle (l. 52)

relax
discuss
associate

k) Power orbit (l. 60)

positions of great influence
jobs with high salaries
departments within the
    government

l) On a completely equal footing with (l. 64)

treated the same as
paid as highly as
treated as politely as

2. Complete each sentence using an appropriate form of the word in italics.

a) *Accompanying*   To the ...... of loud applause, she sat down to chair her first board meeting.

b) *Revealing*   The excellent performance of women on company boards has been a ...... to many men.

c) *Eminent*   She is ...... capable of doing the job when the chairman is away.

d) *Power*   If the Managing Director is sick, the Company Secretary is usually ...... to make the major decisions.

e) *Corporate*   This particular US company was ...... early in the 1930s.

f) *Conceded*   Most women do not want ...... from men; they want to merit responsibility.

g) *Able*   In my business I am ...... partnered by my two sons.

h) *Sensitive*   Being arrogant and thick-skinned our chairman is ...... to criticism or advice.

i) *Value*   Over the years his experience has been ...... to our company.

j) *Value*   He is a highly ...... member of our management team.

k) *Uproot* An ...... employee does not usually make a contented worker.

l) *Opportunity* Many politicians are ...... They exploit every situation without regard for principle.

m) *Deserve* She was a ...... winner of the 'Businesswoman of the Year' award.

n) *Initial* Another law relating to women's rights will be ...... this year.

o) *Acknowledge* She was the ...... brains behind the gang of shoplifters.

p) *Mingle* ...... with businessmen at golf clubs can help the career of an ambitious young executive.

C Language Practice

1. Link these sentence groups using words and phrases selected from the box on the left. Make any other necessary changes.

despite
neither
provided that
in case
even though
moreover
in spite of
with a view to
because of
while
yet
regardless of
as well as
unless
on the other hand

Example: We shall go out. It may rain.
            — We shall go out **despite** the rain.

a) We employ experienced personnel. We do not care which sex they are. *regardless of*

b) Juanita Kreps is an attractive woman. She is also very intelligent. *as well as* *Even though*

c) Women frequently reach top management positions. They do not get much encouragement from men. *Provided that*

d) I have no objection to working under a woman boss. She must, however, be good at her job. *Unless we won't be*

e) We must reword this job advertisement. We may be accused of discriminating against women. *In spite of her*

f) She is brilliant at her job. She is very young and inexperienced.

g) This board of directors shows no concern for the problems of its male workers. It seems to be unaware female workers exist. *Neither does / Moreover* *On the other hand*

h) She is highly emotional. We need more spirit and passion on our board since most of the members are almost senile.

i) Our company shows no interest in promoting women. They are not even keen to employ them. *Neither a* *they*

j) Some people do not appear to work very hard. They earn a lot of money. *despite* *yet*

k) The USA is a country where women directors are common, *while* Saudi Arabia is a country where they are rare. *Unless S*

l) We would not normally appoint a woman to the board. She would have to possess specialist knowledge of some management function.

134

2. Make sentences from these notes.

   a) Men/USA/now used to/women/positions of power/many sectors of the economy.

   b) Even nowadays/women/difficult/get to the top/business world.

   c) USSR/common/women/positions/high responsibility/industry.

   d) Expected/within 30 years/President/USA/woman.

   e) Modern society/progress/improving/work opportunities/all women.

   f) Past/only choice/majority of women/stay at home/kitchen sink.

   g) Many countries/Middle East/husbands/prevent/wives/a job/outside/home.

   h) Most men/not jealous/larger role/women/business life/their countries.

D Oral Work

1. Argue for or against the following debating theme.
'The fact that in many countries the number of women directors is increasing is not necessarily a sign of progress.'

2. Discussion Topics

   a) In the group with which you are now studying, there are probably people from several countries. In these countries, what changes in *company* attitudes towards women are taking place?

   b) Should it be a legal obligation for each company to reserve one seat on its board for a woman so that the interests of the female employees in the company would be safeguarded?

E Writing Exercises

1. You are the Managing Director of a large cosmetics company in your country. For the first time in its history a woman will shortly be appointed to the board. You and your directors have decided to invite the Head of Advertising and Sales Promotion — a female — to join the board team. This person has already been told the decision informally.
It is now your pleasant duty to write a formal but friendly letter to this executive confirming the appointment and indicating what contribution you hope she will make in her new role.

2. Discuss the role of women in the business life of your country, and say in what ways this could be improved.

3. Several different attitudes of women towards their roles as directors are discussed in the text. Summarize the points of view expressed, using about 100–120 words.

Control of Data

Computer operating.

Preparation

1. Give some specific examples of how computers are benefiting modern society.
2. How can the misuse of computers harm either society as a whole or the interests of individuals?
3. What information about yourself should your employer be entitled to keep on file?
4. Have you ever had an improper and unjustified request for information from an official body, e.g. a company, immigration authority, hospital, etc.? If so, give further information about the request.

With the advent of the computer, it has become possible to collect, process, store and disseminate vast amounts of data. This technological advance has made a powerful impact on our daily lives. To give just one example of the beneficial use of computers: if you
5   have a rare blood group, and become involved in a car crash, health authorities can, by using computerized data, quickly locate a blood donor of your group. In the business field, computers have been widely used and have brought obvious benefits. Many of the things we take for granted today, such as swift reservations at hotels or on
10   airlines, just would not be possible without the use of computers.

Like fire, however, the computer is a good servant but a bad master. Its ever-increasing role in our life has created a number of problems, the nature of which we shall now illustrate with some examples. The three cases we mention below show different types of
15   problems associated with computer use or misuse.

—In the USA details of personal medical records, stored in computers, are often leaked to credit investigators and employers. A young businessman from St Louis in the USA recently lost a good job offer because outdated medical data concerning him was
20   passed on to a personnel officer.
—A woman from Detroit received a credit card bill for the amount of $0.00. As this seemed to indicate that she owed nothing, she ignored it. Soon she began to receive monthly, then weekly notices about her unpaid balance. In the end she made out a cheque for
25   $0.00 and sent it off to the company. The letters stopped but then she was charged for late payment of the bill!
—In Holland nearly half a ton of computer tapes were removed from the ICI company there, and used to try to extort a ransom of £27,000 from it. ICI admitted that the cost of replacing the tapes in
30   computing time alone would have been considerable.

These three cases focus our attention on important issues related to the use of computers. Firstly, the individual's right to privacy; secondly, the dehumanizing of relations between the public and

35 business enterprises as a result of computer use; thirdly, computers and criminal activity.

The individual's right to privacy is obviously threatened if a government misuses information stored in the computer banks of its various state departments. If all data from these sources was collated, a government could get a detailed picture of a person's private life,
40 and perhaps use such information to harm that person. To show just how much information might be gained, we give below a chart, taken from *Business Week* (4 April 1977), showing the number of different files in which a US citizen might figure:

17 Federal Files

45	*Where filed*	*Type of file*
	Internal Revenue Service	Tax (1040)
	Social Security Administration	Regular account
	Veterans Administration	Military service record
50	Bureau of Alcohol, Tobacco & Firearms	Gun collections
	Clerk of Congress or Federal Election Commission	Political contributions over $100
	Coast Guard	Boat registrations
55	Defense Intelligence Agency	Executives in companies with military contracts
	Federal Aviation Administration	Applicants for and holders of private plane licenses
60	Federal Communications Commission	Ham operators, boat radio licensees
	Federal Trade Commission	Many top executives, multipurpose files
	Health, Education & Welfare Dept.	Parents of students seeking student loans
65	Justice Dept.	Families of juveniles facing drug or similar charges in a court
	Securities & Exchange Commission	Corporate insiders
70	Small Business Administration	Loan applicants
	State Dept.	Passports
	Treasury Dept.	Banking transactions over $10,000
75	White House	Advisory commission appointees, candidates for federal jobs

Data: Privacy Protection Study Commission

Another worry is that one department, e.g. the Health department, might pass information about an individual to another — say the
80   Inland Revenue or Internal Security department. Many would consider such an action to be an invasion of the individual's privacy.

Linked to the problem of safeguarding privacy is the question of how long data should be kept. Recently, in the US, there was a case involving a businessman who, at the age of 19, wrote a cheque which
85   bounced. Seven years later he was denied credit because of an outdated private credit report.

Laws on data privacy have been enacted in several countries, and others are studying draft proposals on the subject. Sweden and the US probably have most experience in this field.

90   The Swedish Data Act came into effect in July 1974. It introduced the idea of data trespass, making it an offence to obtain data you are not authorized to have. It also provided for a Data Licensing Board. To collect data, a person or organization needs a licence from the board, and this states specifically the purpose for which the
95   information may be used. The Post Office in Sweden, for example, had to ask for a licence to print the telephone directory. In another application, the Reader's Digest publication was refused permission to sell its mailing list.

Perhaps partly because the US has in service more computers than
100 any other country, its public is highly sensitive when questions of privacy arise. Two laws, the Freedom of Information Act (FOIA) and the Privacy Act, apply to all federal record systems, besides computer-based ones. There are, incidentally, about 54 federal agencies, operating 858 computerized data banks containing some
105 1.25 billion records on individuals. The two acts allow individuals to write for copies of personal records collected by these agencies, and, to some extent, to control disclosures of these to other agencies.

However, there are many loopholes in these laws, and the Inland Revenue, for example, is still able to pry deeply into a person's
110 affairs.

There is increasing evidence that computers are leading to a dehumanizing of relations between customers and business enterprises. More and more people are meeting difficulties in dealing with the impersonal machines used by companies to handle
115 paperwork. So great have been the complaints that some companies have taken measures to improve the human links between machines and customers. In the US, for example, the Shell Oil company set up a free telephone line for customers who wanted to sound off about errors in their computerized bill. Other companies have established
120 customer relations offices to add a personal connection between irate customers and the impassive machines which send out the bills.

Computer security is a real headache for many companies. It is, in practice, very difficult to detect acts of embezzlement, fraud or theft where computers are used. The reasons for this are highly technical
125 and outside the scope of this article, however we can give one reason which is relatively easy to understand.

Manual systems of accounting, although dealing with great quantities of documents, nevertheless offer greater security than computerized ones, because the paper goes through many clerical
130 and supervisory levels. This means that if the fraud is to be successful, it must pass the repeated scrutiny of many people. When a computerized system is used, masses of paperwork may be compressed into recorded signals on a single reel of magnetic tape. Clearly, the number of people in the chain is much less. A great deal
135 of information is put in fewer hands, with fewer checks being effected.

Even if companies do get on the track of employees who are committing computer frauds, they are often willing to hush up the matter and suffer in silence. Managements may fear that publicity
140 about internal frauds could affect the share values of their companies in the stock market. Some are so publicity-shy that they do not report such crimes.

Language Notes

Line 28	*A ransom*: a sum of money paid for the release of a person or thing.
Line 59	*Ham operators*: amateur radio operators.
Line 81	*Invasion of privacy*: disturbance of one's right to a private life.
Line 118	*To sound off*: to make complaints. The expression is used mainly in the USA.
Line 123	*Embezzlement*: obtaining money fraudulently.

A Comprehension

1. Explain the statement: 'The computer is a good servant but a bad master'.
2. What point is the writer trying to make by including in the text the chart on page 137?

3. How could government departments misuse information stored in their computers?
4. Why did the Post Office in Sweden have to get authorization to publish their telephone directory?
5. In what way does the US Freedom of Information Act (FOIA) safeguard the rights of the individual?
6. How have companies tried to overcome the problem of 'dehumanized relations' resulting from their computerized systems?
7. Why do manual systems of accounting give a company greater protection against fraud than computerized ones?
8. Explain why an employee who uses a computer for fraudulent purposes does not necessarily face criminal charges when found out by his company?

B Vocabulary

1. Supply words similar in meaning to those italicized in the text, or, if you prefer, briefly explain their meaning.

   a) With the *advent* of the computer, it has become possible to *disseminate* vast amounts of information.

   b) Many things we *take for granted* would not be possible without computers.

   c) The tapes were used as a means of *extorting* a ransom.

   d) The three cases *focus* our attention on important issues.

   e) Laws on data privacy have been *enacted* in many countries.

   f) There are many *loopholes* in the two laws and the Inland Revenue is still able to *pry* into a person's affairs.

   g) Some companies have tried to establish a personal connection between *irate* customers and the *impassive* machines which send out bills.

   h) It is very difficult to *detect* acts of embezzlement when computers are used.

2. Interpretation of words and phrases. Circle the number next to the most suitable meaning of the word in *italics*.

   a) Details of medical records are often *leaked* to investigators.
      (i) offered for payment
      (ii) despatched on request
      (iii) given without authorization

   b) If all data from these sources were *collated* ......
      (i) distributed   (ii) reviewed   (iii) compared

   c) A businessman wrote a cheque which *bounced*.
      (i) He had no funds in the bank.
      (ii) He had insufficient funds in the bank.
      (iii) He did not have an account at that bank.

d) The Inland Revenue is still able *to pry deeply into a person's affairs*. Therefore an individual:
   (i) is not fully protected by the Act.
   (ii) can keep nothing secret from the tax authorities.
   (iii) has no privacy at all.

e) When relations between customers and companies become *dehumanized*:
   (i) there is a lack of human contact between the two.
   (ii) there are not enough human relationships.
   (iii) there are too many humans involved in the chain.

f) A free telephone line was set up for customers who wanted to *sound off* about computer errors.
   (i) enquire   (ii) complain   (iii) inform

g) If companies do *get on the track of* employees committing frauds, they are often willing to *hush up* the matter.
   (i) suspect   (i) delay taking any action
   (ii) accuse   (ii) give the person a warning
   (iii) catch   (iii) keep quiet about what happened

HOME COMPUTER MARKET

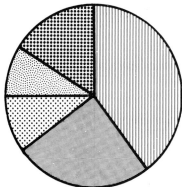

	40% EDUCATION SUPER CALCULATORS
	25% SMALL BUSINESSES
	16% HOME COMPUTER ENTHUSIASTS
	10% MISCELLANEOUS
	9% TECHNICAL SCIENTIFIC

C Language Practice

1. You are the industrial correspondent of an important daily newspaper in Britain. You have just telephoned a friend who works for a magazine called *Everyman's Computer*. He has given you — over the phone — the results of a survey conducted by his magazine concerning the use of 'home' computers in Britain. Here are the notes you hastily wrote as he talked.
   —Home computer market: mainly small microprocessor-based machines, costing up to £1,250.
   —Sales: 1979   15,000 (£10 million)
           1980   25,000
           1981   40,000 (?)
           1982   60,000–80,000 (?)
   —15,000 home computers now in use.
   —325 retail outlets now; 1000 by 1985
   —Next home computer show: Excelsior Hotel, Mayfair, Sept. 8–13. Organized by the magazine.

   Instructions: Using some of the information above and to the left, write a short article which will appear in the Science and Technology section of your newspaper.

2. Rephrase each sentence using the given word.
   Example: He told me how my friend in the States was getting on.
             NEWS
             — *He gave me news about my friend in the States.*

a) He told me how to work the machine.
   ADVICE

b) A team of scientists is looking into ways of using computers in medicine.
   RESEARCH

c) She has shown that computer crime is in fact very widespread.
   EVIDENCE

d) I had never seen such a complex and expensive machine.
   EQUIPMENT

e) He told me many details about how the computer programme
   was prepared.
   INFORMATION

f) For the conference, we hope to stay at the superb Excelsior
   hotel.
   ACCOMMODATION

g) We have not yet had time to evaluate these facts.
   DATA

D Oral Work

1. Argue for or against the following debating themes:

   a) 'The arrival of the computer marks an important stage in the
      increasing dehumanization of modern society.'

   b) 'Computers create employment opportunities rather than
      reduce them.'

2. Discussion Topics

   a) Should employees in a company have a legal right to see *all*
      information that has been included in their personal files?

   b) The car manufacturer, British Leyland, wanted to recall 400,000
      'Marina' cars because of possible faults. It had data of its own
      through which three-quarters of the owners could be traced.
      The government's Licence Centre in Wales had the data on the
      remaining quarter but refused to give it on the grounds that
      this would be a breach of privacy. What do you think of the
      Licence Centre's decision?

   c) 'Child of man's brain, the computer will become his salvation
      in a world of crushing complexity.'
      Discuss this statement.

E Writing Exercises

1. Outline some of the ways in which computers have influenced our
   daily life and comment on the effects, beneficial or otherwise, of
   their use in the activities you mention.

2. The use of the computer and other data storage systems pose a
   serious threat to the individual's right to privacy. Discuss this
   view.

3. 'Computer intelligence is growing at an ever-increasing rate, with
   no natural limit in sight. But human evolution is a nearly finished
   chapter in the history of life.' Discuss.

Equality for Women — Sweden shows how

Preparation

1. What do you understand by the phrase 'equal rights for women'? Can women in your own country claim to possess such rights?
2. Define the term 'male chauvinism'. Give some examples of this based on your own experience.
3. Many people consider Sweden to be a 'progressive' country. To what extent do you agree with this generalization?

It is easy to pay lip service to the idea of equality for women but in practice this is often difficult to achieve. People's attitudes do not change overnight, and it takes time, as well as education and example, to remove prejudice. In many countries women still have
5 great difficulty entering such professions as medicine and law, while the idea of a woman truck-driver or race-horse jockey would be unthinkable.

In Sweden, however, equality of the sexes has been carried far. One reason for this is that there has been a shortage of labour in the
10 country. Unemployment has been low, the population has remained static, so new jobs have had to be filled by women. Nowadays women comprise about 40% of the working population — a high percentage compared with other countries. A second reason is that positive measures, in the form of government action, education and
15 propaganda, have been used to bring about greater equality for women.

Campaigners for women's rights argued convincingly that there were two labour markets in Sweden, one for men and one for

The Swedes are proving that traditionally 'masculine' jobs can be done successfully by women.

women. They stressed that women were mainly gathered in the
20   office, caring and service sectors of the economy. Over 97% of typists
were female, 92% of health service staff and 80% of shop assistants.
Men could choose much more freely amongst a wide variety of
occupations; furthermore, they completely dominated the
manufacturing industries and technical trades.
25   Those sympathetic to women's rights considered that the problem
was to persuade more women to work and, more specifically, to get
women to undertake traditionally masculine jobs.

Some would say the first significant step in Sweden was taken as
early as 1958 when women priests were accepted in the official
30   Lutheran church. Four years later another step was taken. The
principle of equal pay was recognized in a binding agreement
between trade unions and employers. In the 1970s, important
developments took place leading up to the introduction of a
revolutionary scheme to recruit women for men's jobs.
35   In 1972, separate taxation for a husband and wife was allowed. This

Husbands in Sweden are now
encouraged to take a more active role
in child care.

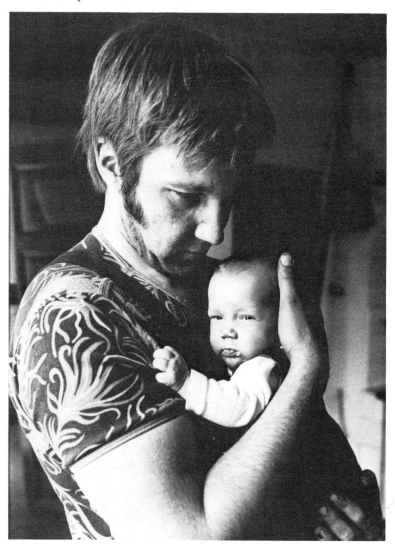

144

created an incentive for women to go out to work. Two years later, a scheme of 'parents' insurance' was brought in. During the first seven months after the birth of a child, either parent could stay away from work, and still collect about 90% of normal pay. The idea was to
40　encourage husbands to take part of this time off. They would then develop closer contact with their children, so it was thought, and take a more active role in child care later on.

Another related benefit was that parents of young children could take off ten days each year to look after them if they were sick.
45　The most far-reaching measures were directed at tempting, even pushing, women into traditionally masculine jobs. Since 1974, companies applying for regional development grants have had to be willing to take on at least 40% of the sex that does not normally dominate their industry. The purpose of this is not only to produce
50　more female lumberjacks, for example, but also more male textile workers; also, employers who provide in-service training for workers in jobs normally held by the opposite sex get a subsidy towards the cost of their wages. Finally, local employment offices throughout the country have taken on extra staff specializing in the problems of
55　women's employment. Part of their brief is to 'prevail upon employers and job seekers to take an unconventional attitude' about appropriate work for their sex.

One programme in particular has attracted international interest. A pilot scheme was introduced, in six of Sweden's twenty-four
60　counties, to persuade women to take on 'masculine' jobs. Areas were chosen where there was a shortage of labour and many unemployed women. Invitations were sent out to all women in these areas, and those interested in working were invited to attend an information day at chosen companies. They were thus given an opportunity to
65　study the manufacturing processes of the local industries. Next, they registered for a four-week course consisting of practical orientation in a certain type of work. At the end of this period many stayed on and were hired by the company. Before this, during their course, they had been paid by the Labour Market Administration, not by the
70　companies.

This experimental programme proved highly successful. It was extended to other counties and eventually involved over 100 companies. It produced women painters, electricians' apprentices, lathe operators, even foundry workers. One 56-year-old woman who
75　got a job grading and marking parts for turbines in a large factory said, 'It was the most wonderful Christmas present which I could ever have received. To get a job at my age is not the easiest matter. When, in addition to this, one has had no previous work experience and is a woman, the matter is in no manner facilitated'.
80　Other measures are in the pipeline. It has been suggested that widows' pensions should be abolished. Alimony payments have been reduced, on the principle that a woman ought to go out and support herself rather than depend on her former husband.

Of course, some problems have arisen. When a wife works a
85　morning shift and her husband an afternoon shift, then they may only really see each other at weekends. Also, many husbands are still reluctant to do their share of household chores even though their wives have full-time jobs. Life can be tough in Sweden for the working woman!

Language Notes

Line 1	*To pay lip service to*: say something publicly but insincerely. The phrase is usually pejorative (has a bad sense).
Line 53	*Part of their brief*: their 'instructions'. An official committee of inquiry is generally given a 'brief' which is incorporated in its 'terms of reference'.
Line 64	*Practical orientation*: many companies have orientation programmes for new staff. The idea is to familiarize new employees with the work of the company as a whole and to help a person adapt to the new work environment.
Line 72	*Lathe operators*: a lathe is a machine for turning wood or metal.
Line 72	*Foundry workers*: a foundry is a place where metal is melted and moulded.
Line 78	*In the pipeline*: in the course of preparation.
Line 79	*Alimony*: maintenance allowance paid to a woman who is divorced.
Line 87	*The working woman*: the definite article is used before a singular noun in this instance to represent a class of persons, i.e. all women who work. We say, for example, '*The* well-informed man buys the *Times*', i.e. all men who are well-informed.

A Comprehension

1. Explain what the first sentence of the text means.
2. What special reason is there for the fact that women in Sweden have made rapid progress towards obtaining equal rights?
3. In what way was the scheme of 'parents' insurance' (l. 35) expected to benefit children?
4. Local employment offices began to hire specialists in the field of women's employment. What, in particular, were they asked to do?
5. What specifically was 'experimental' about the pilot scheme (l. 56)?
6. From a company's point of view, what would be some of the advantages and disadvantages of running such a pilot scheme?

B Vocabulary

1. Interpretation of words and phrases. Circle the number next to the most suitable answer.

   a) The population has remained *static*.
      (i) small in number.   (iii) scarcely changing.
      (ii) gradually decreasing.

   b) Women *comprise* 40% of the population.
      (i) make out   (ii) make up   (iii) take up

   c) Positive measures have been used to *bring about* greater equality.
      (i) reach   (ii) facilitate   (iii) achieve

d) *Campaigners* for women's rights argue . . .
    (i) people supporting a cause
    (ii) people resisting authority
    (iii) people forming a party

e) The principle of equal pay was recognized in a *binding* agreement.
    (i) obligatory   (ii) mutual   (iii) special

f) Separate taxation *created an incentive for women to work*.
    (i) helped them to work.   (iii) encouraged them to work.
    (ii) enabled them to work.

g) Employers providing in-service training get a *subsidy* towards wages.
    (i) financial contribution   (iii) large reduction
    (ii) tax concession

h) Part of the specialist's *brief* is to *prevail upon* employers to take an unconventional attitude.
    (i) instructions   (i) persuade
    (ii) field   (ii) insist
    (iii) interest   (iii) propose to

i) A *pilot* scheme was introduced.
    (i) initial   (ii) experimental   (iii) preliminary

j) The women were given *orientation* in a certain type of work. The purpose of this was to:
    (i) teach them the skills.
    (ii) familiarize them with the job.
    (iii) train them for their duties.

k) Other ideas are *in the pipeline*. This means that:
    (i) other ideas have been discussed.
    (ii) other programmes are about to be introduced.
    (iii) other schemes are being worked out.

l) *Alimony payments* have been reduced. Consequently:
    (i) unmarried mothers are getting less state support.
    (ii) widows are receiving smaller pensions.
    (iii) women are receiving less money from former husbands.

m) When a woman works a morning *shift* . . .
    (i) change of time   (iii) rate of pay
    (ii) period of work

n) Many husbands are *reluctant* to do their share of the household *chores*.
    (i) untrained   (i) repair work.
    (ii) unable   (ii) home decorations.
    (iii) unwilling   (iii) boring tasks.

2. Complete each sentence using appropriate forms of the italicized words.

a) *Prejudice*   many male employers are ...... against women.

b) *Profession*   This job has obviously been done very ......

c) *Equality*   Most socialist governments attempt to reduce ...... in their countries.

d) *Comprise*   It is a complex law ...... four separate sections.

e) *Compare*   In some ways, the position of women in Sweden is ...... to that of women in the USA.

f) *Convincing*   Feminists usually speak with passion and ....

g) *Revolutionary*   Women's rights' leaders in Europe and the US have ...... our society.

h) *Separate*   The two of them are always seen together. They really are ....

i) *Encourage*   There are ...... signs that people's attitudes are changing.

j) *Subsidy*   In some European countries, the wages of young workers are being ....

k) *Prevail*   Groups fighting for women's rights are ...... in the US and Sweden.

l) *Orientation*   When a person begins a new job, he may feel rather ...... at the beginning.

m) *Experience*   Having been in this position for only a month, she is naturally rather ....

n) *Abolish*   The ...... of different pay scales for men and women is our aim.

o) *Support*   His chauvinistic attitude towards all his secretaries is absolutely ....

p) *Tough*   This metal has been ...... by a special process.

C Language Practice

1. Complete the sentences below using appropriate forms of the following auxiliaries: **must**; **would**; **should**; **could**; **need**; **have to**; **to be able to**.
   Note: Some sentences will require negative forms.

   a) It is recommended by the committee that women ...... be given longer vacations.

   b) At the end of the pilot scheme, many of the women ...... get jobs in the companies to which they were attached.

   c) We worded our advertisement carefully to avoid accusations of discrimination, but we ...... bothered because no women applied for the job. They ...... been very impressed by the employment terms we offered.

   d) Some of our directors think we ...... appointed a woman to the board years ago. If we had done so, we ...... avoided the trouble we're now having with female staff.

e) ...... you wish to study this legislation, you can buy copies of the act at government bookstores.

f) To enter certain parts of pubs in Canada, a woman ...... be accompanied by a male. If she made an attempt to go in, the proprietor ...... immediately ask her to leave.

g) It has been proposed that non-working wives ...... be paid a salary by the government to compensate them for their housekeeping responsibilities.

h) Progress towards equal rights has been slower in Britain than in Sweden. It ...... be that British people are conservative, and therefore they ...... make quick changes in attitude.

i) When we were young, we ...... joke with our sister about her boyish looks, but there's nothing boyish about her now!

j) Our company ...... taken on many more females last year, but few women seemed interested in working for us.

k) To become qualified as a doctor, you ...... study for many years.

l) The law in our country ...... changing. It ...... be illegal for an employee to dismiss a woman who is pregnant.

m) If only people ...... realize how unfair it is for a woman to be paid less for equal work.

n) The employment office has urged that more women ...... be interviewed for factory jobs.

o) A woman has been appointed to the Chief Accountant's position. She ...... convinced the interview team she ...... do the job successfully.

2. This exercise gives you practice in using adverbs correctly. For each blank space, supply an appropriate adverb selected from the list on the left. (Use an adverb more than once, if you wish.)

| highly |
| strictly |
| bitterly |
| widely |
| broadly |
| deeply |
| greatly |
| vastly |
| fully |
| firmly |
| utterly |
| totally |
| much |
| entirely |

a) The Swedish progress towards equal rights has been ...... admired by other nations.

b) We are ...... opposed to discrimination against women.

c) The Swedish government is ...... convinced the pilot schemes have been successful.

d) The Swedish prison system is ...... superior to ours.

e) Feminist associations in the US are ...... organized.

f) We were ...... disappointed when we lost our court action.

g) Anyone who thinks women in Britain have equal rights with men is ...... mistaken.

h) Swedish employment practices have been ...... copied in other countries.

i) I am ...... bored by the whole subject of women's lib.

j) The movement for greater women's equality is ...... based in our country.

k) I was ...... distressed to learn she was sick.

l) We are ...... delighted with the success of our campaign.

m) Companies are ...... confused by the new law.

n) I had ...... forgotten I had to meet her.

o) I am ...... covered against all risks.

p) The number of persons permitted to take part in the scheme will be ...... limited.

D Oral Work

Discussion Topics

1. How does Sweden's progress towards women's equality compare with that in your own country?

2. Are there certain jobs which are inappropriate for women to do? If so, which are they?

3. Can a woman combine success in business with success in bringing up children and the enjoyment of a stable family life?

4. 'For many women, the ideas of feminists are profoundly disturbing and even positively harmful.' Discuss.

5. When advertizing a job vacancy, employers should be allowed by law to state their preference regarding the sex and age of applicants. To what extent do you agree with this view?

E Writing Exercises

1. In which country of the world do you feel women have achieved a satisfactory status in society? Outline the reasons for your answer.

2. 'The acceptance of feminist ideas and attitudes by a society leads inevitably to the weakening of marital ties, and therefore to the structure of that society.' Discuss.

Uranium Mining in Australia

Preparation

1. What is uranium used for?
2. What are some of the dangers associated with the mining and distribution of this substance?
3. Why might some Australians oppose the exploitation of the uranium deposits in their country?

Is uranium a blessing or a curse? In the wrong hands it could be as dangerous as a poisonous serpent.

Uranium is the raw material used by nuclear reactors, and so by the electricity-generating industries of the world. When the substance is refined, deadly nuclear weapons can be fashioned from it. Some people see uranium as an indispensable source of energy for a
5   power-hungry world. They want the world's deposits to be exploited as rapidly as possible. Others consider the material to be a threat to world peace. They would like to see this type of mining rigidly controlled, and even banned.

When the Australian Prime Minister, Mr Fraser, officially
10   announced in the summer of 1977 that his government had decided to resume the mining and export of uranium from its Northern Territory, the event attracted world-wide attention. What he was in fact telling the world was that the Australian government would not be leaving almost 25% of the Western world's reserves of low-cost
15   uranium in the ground.

1. **Uranium development in Australia**

a) *How it began*

It was known as far back as 1894 that there was uranium in Australia,
however the search for this material only began in 1944 when the
20   government was asked by the UK to help find uranium for the
Western world's defence needs. Small finds were made at first, then
more substantial ones resulted when the searches became more
systematic. The most important find was the Mary Kathleen deposit
in Queensland. At the time of the Fox enquiry (see section b), it was
25   the only mine in Australia currently producing uranium.

b) *Finds in the Northern Territory*

In 1968, exploration began in what is now known as the 'Alligator
Rivers Uranium Province' in the Northern Territory, east of Darwin.
During 1970 the discoveries of the Nabarlek, Ranger, Jabiluka and
30   Koongarra deposits were made. These newly-found reserves were so
substantial that it soon became clear that the Alligator Rivers Region
was the world's largest uranium province. The Ranger deposit was
the biggest in this area.

    An agreement was reached with two mining companies for the
35   development of uranium mining in the Northern Territory,
beginning with Ranger, but problems arose because the new finds
were in either the proposed 'National Park' area or in the Arnhem
Land Aboriginal Reserve (see map of region).

    Strong opposition grew among the public and the opposition
40   Labour party leader said that the government had 'jumped on the
gravy train' of a technology that would have a maximum life of 50
years, and would produce toxic wastes that would last for a quarter of

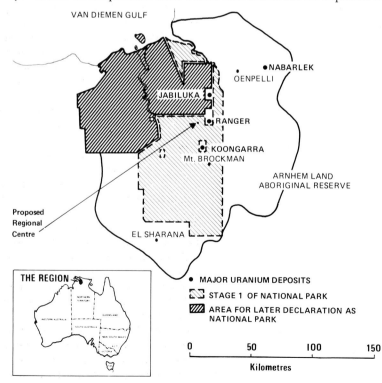

Map showing location of uranium deposits
in the Alligator Rivers region of Australia's
Northern Territory and the site of a
proposed National Park. The mining areas
will be excluded from the National Park,
but included in Aboriginal land. The
Aboriginal people will benefit through
payment of royalties.

a million years. Such strong antagonism, and the fact that no uranium had been mined and exported since 1972, caused the government to
45 commission a public environmental inquiry into the proposal to develop an Australian uranium industry and especially that projected in the Northern Territory. The commission was headed by Mr Justice Russell Fox. The inquiry was based on the study of the Ranger deposit.

50 2. **The Ranger Uranium Environmental Inquiry**
The Commission presented two reports, the second being given to the Australian government in May 1977. These reports covered a number of technical, legal and ethical issues. The main recommendations and conclusions were as follows:
55 — The mining of uranium should be allowed to proceed subject to stringent controls and safeguards.
— Development of the mines should be carried out sequentially, i.e. one at a time, starting with the Ranger deposit. However, the Koongarra deposit should not be developed for the time being
60 since it was in an area of high National Park value.
— The government should suspend mining and cancel sales to countries not conforming to Australian requirements in the use of uranium.
— Uranium mining could become an important industry in national
65 terms, and provide a major source of foreign exchange earnings. Over the period 1981 to 2000, it could bring a gross revenue of £20,000 million and could ultimately contribute 1.3% of the national income in the mid-1990s.
— A fully developed uranium industry could support directly or
70 indirectly 500,000 persons.
— The Commission recommended that land rights should be granted to aboriginals in the area, and they would benefit from any uranium mining. It agreed that the 800 aboriginals in the area were the traditional owners and added, 'the evidence before us
75 shows that the traditional owners, ... are opposed to the mining of uranium on the site'. However the Commission stated bluntly, 'There can be no compromise with the aboriginal position; either it is treated as conclusive, or it is set aside'.

3. **Reactions within Australia to the government's decision to mine**
80 **and export uranium**
When declaring itself in favour of developing the country's uranium resources, Mr Malcolm Fraser's government made it clear that it would be seeking safeguards as to the eventual customers of the material. The conditions of sale would include bilateral treaties
85 between Australia and foreign purchasers, and would involve a written promise that Australian uranium would be used only for peaceful purposes. The government's consent would also be required to reprocess and separate plutonium as a fuel.
    In spite of these safeguards the decision caused widespread protest
90 and sparked off a national debate concerning the wisdom of the decision. Mass demonstrations were held in major cities; environmental pressure groups came out against the decision, as did certain unions, especially those closely connected with the transport of uranium by rail and sea; the Australian Council of Trade Unions

95 (ACTU) called for an interim ban on shipments; the opposition
Labour party wanted to prolong the moratorium on fresh mining and
export of uranium until various safeguards were secured. The major,
controversial issues are now discussed below.

4. Controversial Issues

100 a) *Nuclear proliferation*
Uranium is the material from which plutonium is made, and it is this
substance which is used for nuclear weapons. It is obvious that
countries with nuclear reactors requiring plutonium or highly
enriched uranium could easily divert this material to military
105 purposes, i.e. the making of nuclear explosives. The material could
also fall into the hands of terrorist organizations. It follows, therefore,
that development of the nuclear power industry is unintentionally
leading to an increased risk of nuclear war.

Many Australians argue that their government should only sell
110 uranium to countries which have signed the nuclear non-proliferation
treaty. The Prime Minister, Mr Fraser, argued that Australia's policy
was based on careful selection of the countries to which exports
would be made, together with safeguards mentioned above.

b) *Preservation of the environment and protection of the aboriginal*
115   *peoples in the uranium fields*
Most of Australia's uranium is in Arnhem Land in the Northern
Territory. This is the home of the aboriginal tribes and of species of
plants, birds, animals, and cave paintings, found nowhere else in the
world.
120 The aboriginals have been traditionally opposed to mining,
viewing it as another intrusion by white man into the area in which
they have lived for more than 25,000 years. As one aboriginal leader
has said: 'It is true that the people who are belonging to a particular
area are really part of that area and if that area is destroyed, they are
125 also destroyed'. They have been backed up by environmentalists who
do not wish to see the great natural beauty of the area destroyed and
the aboriginal culture extinguished.

Typical landscape near the Ranger
uranium deposit.

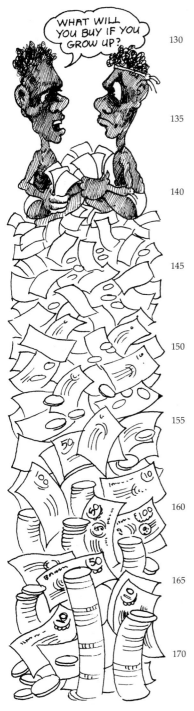

WHAT WILL YOU BUY IF YOU GROW UP?

The government's answer is that it will consider giving land titles to the aboriginals so that they will have some control over the mining. It will also create a national park in this area to protect the physical environment from destruction. The aboriginals of Arnhem Land would get £110 million in royalties over the next 20 years.

c) *Nuclear waste disposal*
Disposal of waste creates problems. Nuclear power stations produce radio-active waste, and if spent fuel is reprocessed, highly radio-active liquid wastes result. The difficulty is to dispose of these wastes in places where there is no risk. Australia is sensitive to this matter because highly radio-active unprocessed waste was dumped at the Pine Gap in the south. The waste came from reactors in Britain, Italy, France and Germany. Immediately people said that Australia was becoming a dumping ground for other countries' waste. The Australian government played down the problem of waste, quoting the advice of experts they consulted: 'None of these authorities has concluded that the use of nuclear energy should be abandoned because of problems associated with waste disposal'.

d) *Dangers associated with uranium mining and its use*
Many Australians spoke up about the hazards associated with the mining and milling of uranium. At the milling stage, the main problem is to make sure that 'toxic seepage' is reduced as much as possible so that plants, animals and humans in the environment will not be harmed.

There is also the danger that miners and those who transport 'yellow-cake' will be exposed to radiation. Many experts claim, however, that uranium mining is not as dangerous as lead mining.

Finally, at the reactor site, the possibility of a major disaster occurring is remote but not non-existent. A nuclear reactor generates intense heat. If both the cooling system and safety devices failed, a terrifying nuclear disaster could be the result.

5. **The case for further development of uranium in Australia**
The pressures on the Fraser government to develop uranium were great. Unemployment was high and there was a shortage of foreign exchange reserves. The value of the Australian dollar had declined. In addition to the employment and foreign exchange arguments, other ideas were put forward in support of the Fraser decision. These were as follows:
— Australia had an obligation to provide fuel for her trading partners who desperately needed it. Its uranium was also necessary to meet the needs of the energy-hungry world at large, and those of the Third World countries in particular.
— By supplying uranium, it would be able to play a more effective role in strengthening safeguards and non-proliferation measures. Furthermore, the development of the 'Fast Breeder Reactor' possibly would not be necessary because enough uranium would be available for the world's needs; fast breeder technology carried increased risks of proliferation.
— Australia could use uranium as a trade bargaining counter. It could, for example, stipulate that uranium supplies would only be made available to EEC countries if it gained higher quotas in Europe for its beef and agricultural products.

180 **Conclusion**

The decision to develop Australia's uranium resources was highly controversial and begs a number of questions. Can one agree with the Australian government that this decision was motivated by a high sense of moral responsibility or does one accept the view of the

185 opposition leader that the Fraser government 'put money before morals'? Should Australia and the rest of the world have left uranium in the ground and concentrated their efforts on harnessing solar energy?

Ought we to accept the advice of one cynic and rush over to visit

190 Arnhem Land while it is still there?

We may be sure of one thing only. When making its decision, the Australian government must have been painfully aware that, in the Australian public's eyes, 'it would be damned if it did and it would be damned if it didn't'!

Language Notes

Line 40	*Jumped on the gravy train*: joined in what seemed to be a profitable enterprise.
Line 90	*Sparked off a national debate*: started; touched off.
Line 96	*Moratorium*: postponement or delaying of a course of action.
Line 142	*Played down the problem*: minimized its importance.

A Comprehension

1. Why did the Australian Prime Minister's announcement in 1977 attract 'world-wide attention'?
2. What really started uranium exploration in Australia?
3. Give some of the reasons for the setting-up of the Fox enquiry.
4. The Fox committee commenting on the aboriginal position said: 'either it is treated as conclusive or it is set aside.' What does this statement mean?
5. What safeguards concerning the use of uranium did Mr Fraser's government envisage? How effective do you think these would be?
6. Define the term 'nuclear proliferation'. Why could development of the world's nuclear power industries lead to it?
7. Aboriginal leaders have talked about the white man's 'intrusion' into their land. What do they mean by this?
8. Why does getting rid of nuclear waste create problems?
9. How would development of Australia's uranium help its trading interests?
10. The Australian government 'would be damned if it did and it would be damned if it didn't'. Explain this statement.

B Vocabulary

1. Provide an appropriate word for each blank space.

   a) During the last year, uranium has been a controversial ...... in Australia.

b) Australia's ...... regarding uranium has been criticized at home and abroad.

c) Scientists and politicians have been trying to find ways of ...... the world's energy needs.

d) Australia decided to resume mining of its uranium ....

e) Uranium is the .... used by nuclear reactors.

f) The report recommended that mining should be allowed, ... to strong safeguards.

g) The government's decision was highly ......, some Australians supporting it, and others opposing it.

h) Many people questioned the ...... of this decision.

i) One problem is that countries supplied with plutonium could easily ...... the material to military purposes.

j) Opponents of the Fraser government wanted a ...... on new mining until certain safeguards had been agreed.

k) As compensation, the aboriginals will receive ...... over a period of 20 years.

l) Some authorities ...... that uranium mining is not a particularly dangerous activity.

m) Because of the economic situation of the country, there was great ...... on the government to resume mining.

n) In trade negotiations, Australia could use uranium as a .... to get concessions from other countries.

2. Complete each sentence using an appropriate form of the word in *italics*.

a) *domination* Japan has been a ...... force in world trade in recent years.

b) *preoccupied* Our sales director, understandably, has a ...... with sales targets and market shares.

c) *search* At the interview they asked me some ...... questions.

d) *resume* It is uncertain when there will be a ...... of talks between the two leaders.

e) *refine* On meeting her, one is immediately aware she is a woman of ....

f) *substantial* The conclusions he reached in the report will need to be ...... by more supporting evidence.

g) *technology* The ...... advances in the uranium mining industry have been considerable.

h) *conclude* There is no ...... proof that uranium mining is more dangerous than many other types of mining.

i) *enrichment* Listening to Bertrand Russell talk was an ...... experience.

j) *sensitive*   Right-wing governments are often criticized for being ...... to the needs of the poor and underprivileged.

k) *authority*   She has written an ...... study on immigration.

l) *value*   It is difficult to ...... his contribution to research because little of his writing is available in this country.

m) *exposed*   Some people find that ...... to new ideas is an upsetting experience.

n) *moral*   It is ...... for a country to supply uranium without any safeguards regarding its eventual use.

o) *cynical*   Only a ...... would argue that Australia will allow the complete destruction of aboriginal land in mining areas.

3. Provide an appropriate word for each blank space.

a) The decision ...... favour ...... mining uranium sparked ...... a national debate.

b) The unions called ...... a ban ...... the shipment of uranium. They were backed ...... by other pressure groups.

c) The government was accused ...... playing ...... the potential hazards associated with the mining.

d) An enquiry was conducted ...... the environmental effects of mining the Ranger deposits. A number of proposals were put ...... by interested groups.

e) Purchasing countries must conform ...... certain requirements before a contract of sale can be drawn ....

f) ...... a larger scale, scientists have been preoccupied ...... the problem of developing nuclear energy. Some see the benefits to mankind ...... being worth the risks.

g) The aboriginals need to be protected ...... the intrusion of the white man ...... their lands, and they seek control ...... how the territory will be mined.

h) Australians are especially worried ...... waste disposal problems. They are also concerned ...... the hazards associated ...... mining operations.

C Language Practice

The passages below lack any definite and indefinite articles. Decide which, *if any*, should fill each blank space.

a) Whatever [1]...... long-term future of [2]...... so-called natural forms of energy such as [3]...... wind, wave and tide, none of them has yet reached [4]...... stage of development which [5]...... nuclear energy had reached 20 years ago.

b) While [1]...... effort should be made to develop [2]...... more promising natural sources, it will be impossible for them to make [3]...... significant contribution to [4]...... energy gap in [5]...... near future.

c) There is [1]...... evidence that [2]...... long-term exposure to low doses of [3]...... radiation can be harmful. However, there is no evidence that [4]...... incidence of [5]...... cancer among [6]...... workforce of [7]...... United Kingdom is higher than [8]...... national average.

d) What is known as [1]...... 'plutonium economy' is probably [2]...... most common source of anxiety to [3]...... general public, particularly in [4]...... age when [5]...... international terrorism is increasing.

e) In [1]...... recently published book, [2]...... professor from [3]...... Australian National University claims to have devised [4]...... process which may lead to [5]...... safer method of disposing of [6]...... radio-active waste from [7]...... nuclear reactors.

D Oral Work

1. Argue for or against the following debating theme:
   'The Australian government has put money before morals.'

2. Discussion Topics

   a) 'Proliferation of nuclear bombs among governments is less of a threat to world peace than the ever-increasing activities of international terrorist organizations.' Comment.

   b) 'What white people have wanted in the past, they've always taken. It is only after they've done so that they've written the epitaphs for the people they've destroyed.' To what extent is this fair comment of the Australian government's treatment of the aboriginals in the Arnhem Land?

   c) Is it ethical of Australia to use its uranium as a bargaining counter in trade negotiations with other countries?

   d) It has been said that if there had never been an atomic bomb, nuclear power could be accepted as less environmentally harmful than burning coal. To what extent do you agree with that idea?

E Writing Exercises

1. 'The arrival of nuclear power at this stage in history is providential, and the risks involved in exploiting it, while not negligible, should be accepted.' Discuss.

2. 'The destruction of the aboriginals is a regrettable fact of history about which we can do nothing.' Discuss.

3. 'The stepping-up of energy from existing nuclear sources is the only alternative to a general decline in living standards.' Discuss.

KEY TO SELECTED EXERCISES

Note: *Answers to exercises marked with an asterisk (*) are suggestions only. There may well be other possibilities which are also acceptable. Students working in a class should discuss alternative solutions with their teacher.*

Multinationals

B Vocabulary

1. a) subsidiaries; affiliates; tariffs; quotas.

   b) economic boom; joint-venture; shareholding; repatriated.

   c) guidelines; legally enforceable.

   d) overcapacity.

2. a) enterprising e) threat   h) worrying   k) untrusive
   b) differentiate f) riches   i) indecisive   l) involvement
   c) basically   g) marketable   j) remotely   m) strategic
   d) tense

3. a) (ii) b) (ii) c) (iii) d) (i) e) (iii)

C Language Practice

*1. a) Companies whose national markets become saturated often decide to set up subsidiaries abroad.

   b) The economic boom of the 1960s led to the rapid growth of multinational activity.

   c) In earlier times, multinationals were regarded as heroes, but now they are viewed with suspicion.

   d) Many countries will only allow foreign investment on a joint-venture basis.

   e) Some people regard multinationals as being a threat to national sovereignty.

   f) Some developing countries are concerned about their dependence on foreign investment in key sectors of their economy.

   g) ITT, the American conglomerate, has been accused of interfering in the political affairs of Chile.

   h) The principle of interaction is well exemplified by a company such as Massey Ferguson.

*2. a) It is somewhat surprising that multinationals, who were once considered heroes, are now regarded as villains.

   b) Whether foreign companies have good or bad intentions, their activities will inevitably be closely scrutinized by host governments.

   c) It worried many Frenchmen that after General Electric had bought up the French company Machines-Bull, France no longer had a computer industry.